The
Creative
Mind

Envision Your Dreams, Create Your Reality

Bobbie Celler

The Creative Mind: Envision Your Dreams, Create Your Reality
Copyright © 2014 Bobbie Celler

For more information visit www.TheCellerOrganization.com

Printed in the United States of America

The Creative Mind: Envision Your Dreams, Create Your Reality
Bobbie Celler

1. Title   2. Author   3. Self-Help/Business

Library of Congress Control Number: 2013913335

ISBN 13: 978-0-615-85387-1

Dedication

*To my wife Katy, who has been on this remarkable journey
from its inception: thank you for believing in me.*

*To my four-year-old daughter Brianna, who looks like me
but is as sweet as her mother inside: you really can accomplish
any dream your heart desires.*

*To my three-year-old daughter Kayla, who looks like her mother
but is as tough as I am inside: you have the remarkable power
to persuade anyone to do anything.*

*To my eleven-month-old daughter Angelica, who is the happiest
little baby and emanates the love of both of us with every smile:
keep smiling no matter what they say to you.*

Table of Contents

Uncovering the Creative Mind

Much has been said lately about the need for creativity and innovation. In the last few decades, we have witnessed dramatic changes in the world. Not only have technologies weakened national and continental barriers but knowledge and information capital has rapidly become the most powerful and most sought-after commodity. Indeed knowledge in the twenty-first century is a valuable resource, and those who acquire it enjoy great power. One needs only to examine companies such as Google, Microsoft, and Apple to appreciate this simple fact. As a result of this relatively rapid and major shift, an enhanced focus on creativity and innovation has occurred. Having information and knowledge is beneficial, but being able to add value and enhance knowledge through new explorations and considerations is exponentially better.

My appreciation of this concept developed over several years as I went through the school of hard knocks. If you have experienced similar challenges in the pursuit of success, don't feel bad because you are not alone. Everyone I know who has attained great success over a sustained period of time has experienced their share of difficulties. It seems bumps and bruises received along the journey to success represent the necessary badges of honor for those who have made it. I think of such challenges as mandatory in some form or fashion since they enable us to refine skills and abilities more conducive to attaining future goals. Of course these talents can also be attained through study, comparisons, and reflective insights. In an effort to save you some of the "hard knocks" I experienced, I am providing these lessons for your benefit within this book.

To some extent my life in terms of success has been somewhat cyclical. As a child I experienced poverty and family struggles as my mother sought to raise my sister and me in the slums of Brooklyn. I was determined to succeed; life circumstances drove me not only to complete college but to do so in three years. Being able to complete college at all was a major accomplishment since I was the first in my family, and doing so in record time increased my confidence that I would succeed.

With a persistent drive to prove my abilities to others, I subsequently attained a law degree believing this was the quickest path to great success. But upon completion I realized the career of law (like most endeavors) had its own setbacks. The starting salary for an attorney averaged $35,000 a year while my school loans well exceeded $100,000. Since I was young, determined, and impatient, these two figures did not seem to match my visions of rapid success. As a result I placed my legal talents on the back burner and searched for more-efficient avenues to satisfy my desires.

Like many individuals at the time, I pursued investments in the real estate market, which seemed to be booming, and I attained a fair amount of wealth in a short period as a result. But also like the majority, I rapidly saw my successes evaporate as the housing bubble collapsed, leaving me nearly penniless. I found myself back where I had started. At least I held a law degree. Even in the worst of times, knowledge remains a valuable resource. I soon joined an established law practice, and within months I was back on my feet. My ambition, determination, and desire for success fueled my climb within the firm, and soon I became one of the top producers in the practice. From bust to boom and around again, I was back on top. Success seemed like a traveling relative who periodically came for a visit but could never stay very long. And this analogy again proved to be accurate.

In April 2010 I found myself without a job, in the midst of marital struggles, and with only $37 available on a credit card. After a disagreement with the law firm, I suddenly found myself unemployed and near rock bottom. As I sat alone, I pondered why success seemed so difficult to maintain. At times I had easily achieved my goals, but repeatedly success had been stripped from me as everything around me changed. Perhaps my struggles were a result of being at the right place at the wrong time. Or maybe I was missing something more profound. In that moment the underlying cause of my repeated failures became clear.

In a single word, my strategy to that point for attaining success had been *duplication*. When I had decided to attain a law degree, I knew attorneys had a high chance of becoming successful individuals. If I duplicated the path they had traveled, success was highly likely. When this failed, I followed the popular path of real estate investing hoping to replicate success through simulating the behaviors of others. While both pursuits had culminated in temporary victories, sustained success remained elusive. My recurring falls from grace resulted from my lack of creativity and innovation. By following the leader, I had been able to duplicate success temporarily, but such efforts are never lasting. In order to enjoy longstanding success, one must constantly seek to enhance value through a creative mind.

In the midst of despair and chaos, I found myself sitting alone in my car trying to determine my next move. Suddenly a sense of calm came over me, and I completely shifted my perspective on how to pursue success. Rather than duplicating the legal practices of other firms and attorneys, I would identify a need within the marketplace and create an area of law to meet that need. Instead of perceiving my current situation as a setback, I would embrace it as a personal challenge and an opportunity to learn. With almost nothing left to lose, I chose to invest in myself wholeheartedly. Either I was going to attain my dreams of success, or I was going to be crushed in the process. This was my "aha" moment.

Before the month of April was over, I had established Celler Law P.A. and created an area of law that represented hospitals in medical claims against automobile insurance companies that refused to pay medical bills. Within a couple of weeks, I had my first client. Soon my single client turned into ten, ten into twenty, and twenty into forty. Over the past three years, my law practice has grown tremendously in size, and so have my interests. My creative concepts in law opened new doors for other areas of success. I am president and managing shareholder of several companies involved in medical billing and emergency recovery services. I likewise founded Bobbie Celler Feeds the World, which connects unused food products in the restaurant industry and urban food distribution centers. My charitable efforts have similarly created new opportunities in the television and entertainment industries, where I discuss legal topics, promote musical artists, and orchestrate celebrity business seminars. In three short years, I have regained and surpassed all measures of my prior successes combined by adopting a completely new mindset.

The creative mindset represents a dramatic shift in how I approach success. Prior to my epiphany, I perceived success as a competition. In order for me to attain a top position, others would have to fail. Assuming others' success strategies were essentially the same, all I needed to do was invest greater energy and determination, and my success would be guaranteed...or so I thought. In applying this concept to my previous law firm, I simply needed to practice the same areas of law but infuse greater energy and assertiveness in comparison to the other attorneys. Indeed such a perspective often works for a time, but the competitive mindset leads to cyclical collapses and always results in limited success. Creativity is the path to long-term success, not competition.

The creative mindset is anything but competitive. The creative mind seeks to grow, expand, and enhance everyone and everything in its path. Once I made this shift in my own mind, everything suddenly changed. Instead of focusing on replicating someone else's actions, I began to develop my own journey according to my own passions. Like each of us, I am uniquely different, and my destiny and potential can only be fully realized if I invest in my personal dreams and desires. Once I embraced my uniqueness and creativity, new perspectives appeared as well as new opportunities. In essence I had been liberated from the confinement of the competitive mind and invited into a world of possibility, imagination, and infinite success. This is the power of the creative mind.

Unlike many books that address the topic of success, this book seeks to provide a practical, action-oriented guide to developing a creative mind and enjoying the success you are meant to have. Rather than discussing a variety of metaphysical topics and hoping for success to find you, cultivating success demands action. Positive thinking can be empowering, but if you fail to follow through on these thoughts with tangible efforts, the magnitude of success possible will be significantly constrained. You may have all the necessary components in a matchstick to create fire, but unless you actually strike the match, the flame will remain a dream. Even with the creative mind, success requires action.

For this reason each chapter of this book covers an essential characteristic of the creative mind with practical exercises and activities to help you develop specific skills and perspectives related to success. After thorough discussion of a specific aspect of the creative mind and its necessity in success development, a group of daily to weekly activities are included that typically take just a few minutes to complete. The power of these exercises is not necessarily in the time required to complete them but in your commitment to perform them day after day, week after week. Ultimately, by committing to these practices, you will develop a creative mind that in turn will attract great success in your future.

One important caveat noted in this book pertains to the need to attend to all the essential features of the creative mind. Though each chapter deals with one particular quality, performing the exercises and activities related to just one or a few sections will provide only limited change in your life. For example, positive thinking and encouraging your ability to dream will result in greater confidence and a strong mental attitude, but they are unlikely to produce true success by themselves. These efforts may even attract success opportunities into your life. However, failing to attend to the other components of the creative mind will result in a less than optimal result regardless. In an effort to obtain the most out of this book, appreciate how all the characteristics of the creative mind operate in total. In this particular instance, the sum far outweighs the power and potential of its individual parts.

As you journey through the book, you will find it is structured to start with foundational concepts related to the creative mind followed by increasingly practical aspects related to success realization. For example, early chapters address positive thinking, the law of attraction, belief, faith, and determination. Subsequent chapters then discuss planning, branding, marketing, working your plan, and managing obstacles. Interestingly the creative mind operates in a very similar way. Initially it enjoys a vast landscape in which to ponder conceptual possibilities, but eventually a creative solution is devised that is progressively refined and implemented to make success possible. While you may consume the information in any single chapter as a standalone topic, reading the chapters in sequential order may offer the best approach to develop a creative mindset.

As for myself I have fully embraced the creative mindset and am living proof of how the creative mind can foster unimaginable success within a short period. My current dream is to share these incredible wisdoms with you so you may reap the benefits of a success-filled life and realize your own destiny of success. If you following the principles outlined in this book with passion, dedication, and determination, I have no doubt you will enjoy incredible success within three years just as I have. In the depths of despair and with a mere $37 of credit to my name, I chose to embrace my creative mind and invest 100 percent in myself. And while I have experienced many challenges along the way, the journey has been and continues to be absolutely amazing. I wish for you to share the same incredible experience by cultivating a creative mind and realize your grandest dreams for success. Each of us has this potential. All it takes is the decision to embrace the creative mind.

Chapter One

The Creative Mind: The Power of the Unseen

Why do some people attain success easily and others struggle to get ahead? This is the essential question this book seeks to answer. While many may describe natural talents, education, and fortuitous opportunities as being the reasons, none of these provides consistency in predicting success.

However, an answer does exist. This chapter aims to describe the most basic, fundamental concept underlying success. Nearly every individual who has ever attained success in life has benefited from this concept. Alone this concept may not bring dreams and desires into reality, but combined with the other essentials outlined in this book, it cannot fail. The concept is quite simple, yet it can be incredibly elusive. Likewise it may be difficult to appreciate due to its lack of tangibility. However, it is by far the most powerful source of success ever known, and without it we are hard-pressed ever to reach our potential in life.

In this chapter we will explore the power of the creative mind, the power of the unseen, and the result of positive thinking. These provide the foundation of all success.

Negativity, Fear, and Worry—
A Pervasive Perspective

A few weeks ago, I was walking past a neighborhood park. The sun was shining brilliantly in the mid-afternoon sky. Kids ran, climbed, and jumped from one jungle gym to another without a care in the world while parents sat at the periphery, carefully monitoring the situation.

Suddenly one of the mothers yelled across the playground to her son, "Trevor! Be careful! I don't want you falling and breaking an arm." I looked over and saw the boy the mother had addressed. Consumed in a fantasy world of imagination, he stood on a gym platform, adorned with a makeshift red cape, looking over the edge, contemplating his jump. The boy was no more than five years old. The height of his jump, at maximum, was three feet. An interesting thought struck me about the situation. The mother, out of love and concern for her son, wanted to protect him from harm. In contrast Trevor had little fear of heights and desperately wanted to "fly" while his cape rippled in the breeze.

Trevor's thoughts were saturated with excitement, exploration, and enjoyment while his mother's thoughts were consumed with fears and worries. How could the mother and son perceive this rather mundane task of jumping off a jungle gym so differently? Some might believe the reason was due to maternal instinct and natural parental concern. But the types of thoughts each held within their minds were likely more relevant to their reactions. I am not necessarily suggesting Trevor should have jumped or that his mother should not have warned him of the potential repercussions. But appreciating the types of thoughts we carry in our minds moment to moment is critically important to success.

As children most of us had little to no fears. In our hearts and imaginations, we believed we could achieve any dreams we wanted. Our dreams ranged from being president of the country to being an astronaut or an athletic superstar. All dreams seemed feasible in our childish minds. But very few of us carried these dreams into adulthood. Something happened along the way. Slowly negativity, doubt, and fear took over our minds, replacing the positive and courageous thoughts that once guided us in our youth.

These occurrences represent the downfall of the creative mind.

Through life experiences we often develop increasing levels of fear. Suppose Trevor jumped and skinned his knee. The next time he would perhaps be a little less courageous and a little more cautious. His mother's fears and worries would be reinforced, causing her to continue her pattern of being overly cautious with Trevor's activities. As we experience loss or a negative outcome, the chances that fears and anxieties will subsequently develop become greatly increased. Unless we are conscious of the thoughts we choose to think, these negative considerations gradually paralyze us, handcuffing our creative abilities. More importantly these negative perspectives actually attract the very things we fear.

Fears arise from a variety of experiences we encounter as we move from childhood into adulthood. Socially each of us wants to connect with other people, belong to a group, and fit in to social norms. We fear being isolated and alone. In order to alleviate these fears, we begin to play it safe. An opinion contrary to mainstream ideas may remain locked inside to avoid risking embarrassment or ridicule. A major accomplishment may barely be mentioned for fear of appearing boastful or too lofty in our attempts to connect with others. Ultimately these fears drive us toward the average, preventing us from realizing our potential and fulfilling our personal destiny.

Our uniqueness lacks an opportunity to shine.

Perhaps one of the greatest fears is the fear of failure. We might say, "What if I try to start my own company and it fails? The people where I work now will certainly get a good laugh." Or maybe we say, "But what if I can't make it on my own? I'll not only be without a job but will have blown my savings as well."

Fears and worries go hand in hand with negative thoughts that prevent us from taking risks and pursuing our dreams. Interestingly the biggest risk we can ever possibly take is allowing someone else to determine our fate. Compare the dedicated employee who worked for a company for twenty years to an entrepreneur. The employee, on many occasions, chose to forego entrepreneurial dreams in exchange for the stability of the current situation only to lose his job later. The entrepreneur, on the other hand, took the risk and perhaps failed a few times but eventually realized his or her dreams.

Which one took the larger risk overall?

At the heart of negativity and fear are selfishness and egocentrism. There is an old adage stating that when a person is in their twenties, they are concerned about others are talking about them; when a person is in their forties, they no longer care that people are talking about them; and when a person reaches their sixties, they realize people had never been talking about them from the beginning. The ego has a natural tendency to fill the mind with thoughts of negativity, doubt, worry, and fear. Its desire to protect us from harm fills our thoughts with "what ifs" and "that's impossibles." But when we allow our ego to take control of our mind, we limit our standards and constrain our potential.

This chokes the creative mind.

In today's world negativity is everywhere. Media uses fear to attract audiences because they have realized the vast majority of people crave news and information to appease their internal worries. Watch a news program and count the number of negative versus positive stories. Examine advertisements and see how many lead with a fear or concern and then offer the remedy. Allowing negative thoughts and fears to control your mind is easy. Being passive and supposedly playing it safe takes little energy but risks everything important. Obstacles, when they develop, are perceived as justifications for these fears but instead should be seen as opportunities for growth and success.

These are the very situations that stimulate creativity. In a world full of anxiety and worry, many succumb to fearful paralysis. The first step in reversing this paralysis and traveling down a path toward success involves shifting how we think from negative to positive. Only then can we allow the creative mind and the power of the unseen to pave the way for our dreams to become reality.

Positive Thinking— A Powerful Force for the Creative Mind

Why do some individuals seem to fall naturally into success and others perpetually struggle in poverty and lack of achievement? Is it due to education? Probably not considering many wealthy and successful individuals lacked traditional education. Henry Ford, for example, had very limited schooling. Thomas Edison had only three months of formal education in his entire life.[1] Is the difference related to success a result of environment? This is doubtful since successful individuals have varied backgrounds socially, economically, and otherwise. Maybe it is due to simple luck and being at the right place at the right time. Hardly. In reality anyone can be wealthy and successful no matter what their situation. But it does require two key ingredients from the start: a creative mind and positive determination.

Before discussing positive thinking as an essential component of creativity, one important caveat should be noted. Positive thoughts alone are not enough to realize success. Choosing to think positive thoughts, focusing on positive emotions and repeating self-affirmations, is the only way to shift perspectives and to attract greater creativity and success. However, as this book will demonstrate, planning and action are also required. Nonetheless, success does begin with how we think.

Positive ideas and thoughts in our minds are the seeds of creativity and success that when nurtured with passion, determination, and action, flourish and thrive. By the same token, negative thoughts serve as the foundation for failure when given similar energies.

How can this be true? How can thoughts and ideas hat are intangible, elusive concepts have such powerful effects?

From a simplified perspective, ideas and thoughts shape subsequent events through the law of attraction. Negative thoughts attract negative circumstances while positive thoughts attract positive, beneficial occurrences. The law of attraction is similar to any other natural law and thus reflects a consistent and reliable foundation upon which success can be achieved. In other words the law of attraction is no different from the law of gravity in terms of its reliability. Repeatedly numerous authors have shown how hundreds of successful individuals have utilized the law of attraction in achieving their dreams.[2] While the "how" of this natural law may not be exactly known, science has provided some clues demonstrating how positivity can affect subsequent outcomes.

Barbara Fredrickson, a doctorate professor in psychology, has dedicated her life's research to studying the effects of positive emotions and thoughts on individuals. After developing objective measures to quantify positive and negative thoughts and emotions, she has conducted numerous studies evaluating why some individuals have greater success than others.[3] In many of her studies, a positivity ratio of patients who thrive under treatment is compared to the ratio of those who unfortunately languish. This ratio compares the number of positive emotions experienced daily over a long period of time divided by negative emotions. Consistently she has found that a positive ratio exceeding three to one detects those who will thrive while ratios below this identify those who do not. Several other researchers have reproduced her findings.[4]

Frederickson suggests that positive emotions and thoughts influence many biological processes within our bodies. These influence not only hormonal aspects, providing opportunities to thrive, but also actual changes within brain cells and other organ systems via nervous system connections.[5] In addition physicists have found that what appears to be empty space within atoms is actually tiny packets of energy known as *quantum energy*. Positive emotions and thoughts could easily influence how these energy packets behave, changing the frequency and size of their wavelike patterns.[6] While the exact mechanisms of interaction have yet to be fully defined by science, preliminary evidence does support the law of attraction. In addition it provides logical explanations for how something invisible to the eye can harbor enormous power.

Consider this example of how a creative mind with positive thoughts can attract a change toward success. I know an owner of a tanning salon who repeatedly complained her business was stagnant. Derogatory comments were constantly being made concerning the location, clientele, economy, and so on. The salon would profit only approximately $75 a day. The owner had come to expect this amount and nothing more because in her mind nothing more was possible. Her creativity and ability to think expansively were blocked.

After I had lunch with her, she promised to raise her

expectations for the following day regarding the tanning salon's income. Instead of $75 she would focus on a larger number and think only positively about how that amount would be earned the following day. The amount she chose was $250. Amazingly, the following day, a client purchased product supplies from her allowing this figure to become reality. This story is absolutely true.

A creative mind and positive thinking can attract magnificent things in your life. But just as seeds require water and nutrients to grow, thoughts and ideas require nourishment as well. Many of these ingredients will be discussed throughout the chapters of this book. Two of the most powerful are determination and persistence.

Determination provides the psychic energy enabling an idea not only to come to life but also to persevere through any obstacle. In fact no one can stop a person who is truly determined and willing to sacrifice everything for an idea. We see this in professional sports all the time. Athletes will their way to victory against all odds because of their determination. Similar stories involving soldiers, politicians, entrepreneurs, and those afflicted with illness also support this claim. If someone is willing to do something or die trying, you had better move out of the way.

The interesting thing about determination is its ability to take a positive thought and creatively advance it into reality.

Creativity is the child of positive thinking. Nothing ever develops of out negativity as creativity and innovations are squashed under a mountain of fear and doubt. But positive thinking allows the creative mind to flourish, finding new ways to overcome challenges and envisioning new paths yet to be explored. Determination forces these creative doors to open, and no matter how many barriers and setbacks may occur, a solution will be found. The combination of positive thinking, creativity, and persistence lies at the heart of all success and fosters the development of a truly creative mind. Tapping in to this power is the means by which anyone can achieve the success they want in any area of their life.

Psychic Energy and Realizing Wealth

For most of us understanding how to develop a creative mind can be difficult to grasp. The first thing most of us do when considering a goal is plan out the possible steps that might lead to that goal. For example if our goal is to acquire a million dollars within six months, then we will consider how that might feasibly happen. Perhaps we might win the lottery, or maybe a wealthy relative might leave us an inheritance. But short of these unlikely happenings, we probably would not see a logical path to attain the million dollars. We allow our thoughts to explain why the goal cannot be achieved. We have to see the cause in order to believe in the effect. The problem lies in the way we go about the process. We believe in the goal only if we can define a reasonable sequence of steps toward it. However, instead of focusing on the path, we should focus on the outcome.

The creative mind accepts the dream as reality without necessarily knowing the "how" of the process. Making a plan of action and following that plan toward the goal is important, but each step does not have to be fully defined or known in advance. The most important aspect is simply believing the goal will be attained.

A creative mind supported by strong beliefs is what empowers the law of attraction even more. When we infuse these beliefs with desire and passion, success becomes more readily attainable. Circumstances will occur paving the way toward the goal, and often these fortuitous events could never have been foreseen by our limited perspective. Just because we cannot envision the link between cause and effect does not mean the law of attraction does not exist. In order to develop a creative mind and enjoy the power of the unseen, we must take a leap of faith and believe the outcome will truly happen.

In considering how the creative mind brings about success, one must consider the phenomenon of psychic energy. Also known as thought energy, this has been a longstanding belief among many ancient monistic religions that believe a single unified source of substance and essence permeates all things. For the purposes of this book, we will call this the Creative Source. Buddhism, Hinduism, and several other religions support such perspectives, and through quantum theory science provides support for such beliefs as potential reality as well. If ideas and thoughts are composed of energy waves, then changes in thought types could very well alter the frequencies and amplitude of these waves. We would then attract similar energies in structure toward ourselves as a result of this shift. Negative thoughts would attract others who shared negative opinions while positive thoughts would attract individuals with more favorable outlooks.[7]

Despite the ability to see how psychic energies could attract circumstances toward us, each of us has experienced its effects from time to time. In relation to others to whom we are close, we often experience the phenomenon of knowing one another's thoughts even before they are spoken. Spouses, siblings, business associates, and team members often anticipate one another's thoughts. While this may in part come from shared experiences and familiarity, a sixth sense, so to speak, exists that helps like minds align more readily. Another example of this psychic energy involves an immediate sense of knowing another person despite being recently introduced. When thoughts are well aligned,

positive or negative, the psychic energy between these two individuals creates an instant connection that otherwise would take a
much longer time to develop.

Of course we do not consciously examine whether or not our
psychic energy aligns with another person's or with a particular
environment. Psychic energy connections occur at a subconscious
level. Without knowing it we are attracted to people who share
similar thought energy frequencies as our own and vice versa. I
first noticed this when I began to shift my own set of thoughts
from a negative focus to a positive one. People in my life who
were critical, negative, and fearful suddenly had little in common
with me. The relationships changed rather quickly; a void was left
that soon filled with new relationships. These new relationships
involved individuals who naturally had brighter perspectives.
Interestingly I did not seek to distance myself from my old
acquaintances, and I did not seek new friends or colleagues. The
change simply happened naturally and without effort as I shifted
the energies of my own ideas and thinking. Without question the
creative mind provides great opportunities to attract success in
our direction.

Another fascinating story describes how these psychic energies manifest into reality even when we are completely unaware
they are at work. Many years ago my wife and I were driving
along the beach in South Florida. We came across a magnificent
mansion on the ocean with a circular stone driveway, a central
fountain, arched doorways, and intricately designed window
casements. Deep down I dreamt of one day owning a house just
like that one. Years passed, and my wife and I had not only seen
several houses since then but had lived in a few different ones as
well. Eventually we began looking for the home we planned to
live in for the rest of our lives. After looking at several, we finally
decided on a beautiful home well away from the ocean.

As I was getting ready to close on the house, something reminded me of that mansion by the sea from years past. For no reason other than curiosity, I searched the Internet for the beachfront mansion. To my amazement the home looked nearly identical to the home my wife and I were buying. Even more surprising was that the same builder had designed both homes! Without being conscious of my previous desires, my subconscious psychic energies had attracted circumstances in my life that led me to nearly the same house. Thoughts are powerful, and if we truly desire success we have to appreciate the power a shift in our thinking can wield.

The creative mind and the law of attraction may sound like magic and superstition, but psychic energies do exist. As mentioned science is revealing increasing evidence to support the existence of these invisible forces. In addition the benefits of utilizing the creative mind in attaining wealth, success, health, and a variety of deep desires in life have been demonstrated time and time again.[8] As our thought energies focus on our dreams and our ability to have what we desire, we naturally set in motion a set of events attracting circumstances to make these dreams become tangible. Positive thinking combined with true belief influences other people to behave differently and attracts new individuals into your life while enhancing your creative mind. These events then trigger additional circumstances, and ultimately we achieve the goals and dreams we want.

How to Utilize the Power of the Creative Mind

When our environments are saturated with negativity, fear, and worry, shifting from the negative to the positive can be difficult. Quite frankly negative thoughts are easier than positive thoughts.

They require less energy on our part. For example thinking of all the reasons why a plan will fail, a dream will never come true, or a goal is unattainable is much less complicated than devising the steps necessary for their success or being determined to see past every obstacle.

Creativity demands an infusion of energy. In some strange way, we gain a false sense of empowerment when we can see the flaws existing within a plan. By identifying them in advance, we feel we have outsmarted fate and avoided yet again another disappointment in life. In reality, however, we haven't tricked fate at all. By suppressing the creative mind, all we have done is limit our own potential and robbed ourselves of all the wealth and success we could have achieved. What we knew as children is still true as adults. The sky is truly the limit. We can have everything we desire if we simply exercise our creative minds and believe.

At the very foundation, our ultimate success begins with an idea, a dream, and a thought. These powerful bundles of psychic energy have the potential to move mountains. Many of the world's most successful individuals have realized this simple fact. Nurture an idea with desire, determination, and belief, and that idea will grow in strength to the point that nothing can prevent it from becoming realized.

Having faith in the idea, devising a plan of action, and implementing that plan provide the subsequent steps, but it all begins with our thoughts. We can either choose to think positive thoughts that bring us powerful success, or we can focus on the negative. You are what you think, and choosing to think with a creative mind provides the pathway to success.

But how do we shift our thinking from negative to positive when we naturally gravitate toward the negative? Is it enough simply to tell ourselves to look on the bright side? While this is important, the ability to use positivity in our lives to realize our dreams takes practice. Like with many things, how we think is habitual. When we become accustomed to seeing the world through a certain lens, reframing our perspective in a different light becomes challenging. Consider the person who sees everyone at work as competitors. Regardless of whether the issue is a salary raise, praise for good work, or a promotion in position, colleagues are viewed as competition to one's own success. When everything in our thinking supports this view, it becomes nearly impossible to think of others as creative resources and support. Positive thinking provides the fuel necessary for the creative mind while negativity squashes its abilities every time.

The power of the unseen resides in the creative potential of our minds. Each of us has unique creative abilities that can generate powerful ideas. When we support these ideas with positivity, they flourish. Placing belief and passion behind these ideas is like putting them on steroids. By tapping in to the Creative Source that exists in all things and above all things, ways of perceiving how such ideas can be ultimately realized become apparent. All of these aspects of success will be discussed in subsequent chapters along with practical ways to adopt such behaviors in our lives.

For now realize that success begins with the way we think. If we want to attract success, we must adopt and foster a creative mind.

In order to make the shift from negativity to positivity, pessimism to optimism, and reluctance to determination, committing to several practical actions can help us develop a routine that eventually evolves into healthy habits of success. Whether you desire incredible wealth, a lasting relationship, a new career, or greater health, these steps to positive thinking and a creative mind will unleash the power to realize your goals and dreams. No matter how many setbacks and failures you have experienced, success is accessible to everyone. Each of us has the power to attain the dreams we desire. This is the power of positivity and the creative mind. By believing we can achieve our dreams, we attract circumstances that pave the way for this reality. By pushing aside our fears, doubts, and worries, we distance ourselves from negative situations that deter us from our goals. Positivity fosters our ability to create whatever future we desire, and like Trevor we seize the moment to jump and fly knowing success is within our reach.

Practical Steps toward Achieving the Creative Mind

Appreciating the power of the creative mind and positive thinking begins your journey toward realizing your true potential, your dreams, and your destiny. But how can one adopt a creative mindset of positive thoughts and emotions? If the world is filled with negativity, and life's past experiences have served to create fear and doubt, how can one embrace positivity and nurture creativity? It's easier than you might think, but it does require an investment in effort and energy.

- *Positive Affirmations*
  (five minutes three times daily)
  Survey the thoughts going through your mind on any given day. In all likelihood many are negative commentaries about your abilities, events that will occur that day, opinions others may have, etc. This negative background of thought filled with doubts and fears attracts more of the same into our lives. Therefore the first step is to begin to change this background noise into thoughts that are more positive in nature.
  Positive affirmations are an excellent way to

accomplish this. Take the time to write down several
brief positive statements that can be easily recited.
These may describe your positive attributes, your
determination to succeed, recent accomplishments,
and more. When you recite these to yourself three
times or more daily, your mind not only adopts these
thoughts into beliefs but you will attract positive
circumstances to your life that reinforce these affirmations. Likewise make an effort to erase every negative
thought by replacing it with a positive affirmation.
When you continually make this effort, your thought
patterns will change from negative to positive within
a few weeks.

- ***Distancing from Negativity***
  (five minutes at the end of each day)
  "You're only as good as the company you keep,"
  according to the familiar quote. Nothing could be
  truer concerning negativity and positivity. If you are
  surrounded by people who complain, criticize, point
  fingers, and carry dismal outlooks, avoiding the same
  tendencies will be incredibly difficult. After all like
  attracts like, and negativity will draw you closer to
  its noose the more you are exposed to it. In order to
  immerse yourself in positive thoughts and emotions,
  distancing yourself from negative perspectives and
  individuals is essential. In some instances this may be
  relatively easy. However, when close friends, family
  members, and sometimes even significant others constantly reflect a negative view of the world, distancing
  may be a challenge.
      In order to practice this step toward positivity,

take a few minutes at the end of every day to reflect on negative influences in your life. Which individuals are constantly seeing the glass as half empty? Who is always finding the problems rather than the solutions? Identify these individuals and make an effort to distance yourself from them, from the situation, or from the negative sentiments. For example if a colleague at work always finds fault with a project plan, develop replies and responses that neutralize these negativities with positive spins. As a result one of two things will happen. Either your positivity will begin to influence the other person beneficially, or that person will find your positivity uncomfortable or possibly even irritating. In both situations the negativity moves farther away from you, leaving you with a positive and creative mindset.

- *Shift Your Expectations*
  (five minutes every morning)
  When you approach a challenge, do you assume you will succeed? What are your expectations concerning your abilities moment to moment? Our psychic energies are significantly influenced by the level of expectations we have. If we expect to succeed, we naturally raise the power of positivity within our minds. If we expect to fail, the opposite happens.
    By taking a few moments before the start of each day, you can shift your expectations about what you will accomplish that day. In doing so you invest energy into the outcome, increasing its likelihood of success. And if failure should occur, you make the commitment beforehand to persevere and learn from the

experience. By positively shifting your expectations about the outcomes of specific challenges, you naturally infuse positive energy into your thoughts and feelings. And as successes follow (as they certainly will), these higher expectations will be increasingly reinforced.

- ***Read Motivational and Inspirational Materials (ten minutes daily)***
  You are what you eat, and for your brain you are what you see, read, and hear. The term *garbage in, garbage out* epitomizes this perspective. The more negativity we consider, the more negative our thoughts and emotions will be.

  Instead of reading articles and news stories reporting the gloom and doom of the world, seek out materials that highlight new opportunities, growth, and success stories. Rather than watching television programs investigating the most recent murder, political scandal, or white-collar crime, watch documentaries describing how other successful people overcame great odds to attain their positions in life. Making a conscious effort to feed our minds with positive material is important in adopting positive thinking and emotions. We want to expose our minds to empowering stories and visuals rather than ones that incite fear and worry. Choose to surround yourself with positive messages as much as possible, and invest in reading positive articles or books for at least ten minutes a day. You will be amazed by what this simple task does for your mental health.

- *Positive Action Reinforces Positive Thought*
  (five minutes daily)
  Lastly, positive thinking is interconnected to positive actions. One can adopt positive thoughts all day long; but unless these are accompanied by positive action, a growth mindset toward success is unlikely to reach its potential.

  In addition to your positive affirmations, write specific goals and dreams you want to achieve. Focus on these with a positive attitude, knowing you will attain them as you attract circumstances to your life, making them become reality. Then write down how you will go about accomplishing these goals and dreams. Finally, act on these steps leading toward your goal.

  The pursuit of your dreams through action creates belief and faith in your success, and these are powerful in reinforcing and perpetuating positive thinking. You don't need to know all the steps involved to achieve your goal; you need to devise only the first few. Through positive thinking and the law of attraction, the subsequent steps will reveal themselves as you continue to take action.

  Every evening before retiring for the night, take five minutes to devise several steps you will take the following day toward your goals. As you think of them, accept that they will be done and will further your success. Positive actions provide the feedback necessary to strengthen positive thinking and creativity; when mixed with desire, determination, and faith, they are absolutely unstoppable.

Negative thoughts unfortunately come naturally, but positive thinking can be accomplished through the above steps. When you simply practice these exercises for minutes a day, your thoughts and emotions will change for the better. Before long positivity will be habitual, and you will soon witness the positive circumstances and events creativity attracts into your life. Through these steps you too can realize a shift toward positive thinking in your life. In turn you will begin to reap the benefits of a creative mind that follow and the power of the unseen.

Chapter Two

Unleash the Creative Mind: Dare to Dream

The creative mind lies at the heart of success. But how do we unleash its abilities and its incredible power? The intangible, invisible power of psychic energies holds the key, as we have discussed. These energies not only begin our journey toward success but also pave the way for continued fulfillment throughout our lives. Thus the start of the climb begins with a single idea, a hope, a dream.

For this reason alone, each idea and dream we have deserves careful attention. Think of each one as a delicate seed that needs nurturing so it may expand, grow, and become its greatest possible potential. When we fail to consider our dreams as possibilities, we deprive them of the very energies and environments they need. But when we allow them to flourish in the garden of a creative mind, their potential is limitless. All we have to do is open the doors of our minds to consider that the impossible is possible and that every idea can become reality given the right setting. Above all we must dare to dream.

Dreams and Ideas—The Foundations of Success

As a lecturer and educator, I often hold many seminars. On occasion I may share the stage with gifted speakers who provide complementary messages to the materials I am conveying. On one occasion I found myself sharing the platform with a director of human resources, waiting to speak to an audience of college students about their careers, their ability to attain success, and, of course, fulfilling their dreams. The other speaker started the seminar talking about practical strategies in examining the occupational landscape, assessing one's talents, and more. As I sat patiently waiting for my turn, I intently listened to what the gentleman had to say. Most was sound advice, but then he admitted something about himself that surprised me. He stated, "No one dreams of becoming a human resources director. It's just something one falls into. But I have attained a position I enjoy by taking these important practical steps along the way."

Who was he trying to convince—the students or himself?

What the lecturer basically acknowledged was that he had at some point given up on his own dreams. This had nothing to do with being a human resources director. In fact many individuals in his position dreamed of empowering people and organizations through innovative, creative human-resources strategies. But based on his own statements, this had not been his ultimate dream. In all likelihood he had desired something else and settled for the position of human resources director. By social standards he might have been very successful in terms of status, income, possessions, and more. But somewhere along the way, he had given up on his dream, and with that his ability to achieve his greatest potential of success had vanished. His creative mind, which at one time had been open, expansive, and wild with energy had been tamed, constrained, and quieted.

Today we carry around electronic devices the size of our palms that harbor more computing power than a building full of computers in the 1960s. Space travel, satellites, and space stations provide tremendous amounts of information about our universe that was essentially unknown a few decades ago. Athletes continue to break world records in a variety of sports year after year, many of which were believed to be unbreakable. As amazing as each one of these is, every single accomplishment began with a common source. Individuals like Steve Jobs, Bill Gates, John F. Kennedy, Neil Armstrong, Michael Jordan, Roger Bannister, and many more each had an idea, a dream, and a vision. Without this foundational source of psychic energy, none of the amazing things mentioned would have been accomplished. Without the capacity to dream and, more importantly, the ability to believe in dreams, many modern-day human successes would have yet to be realized.

By some estimates the human brain has approximately 125 billion neurons on average, and each of these forms a complex pattern of connections enabling a vast array of brain-related communications to occur. In fact more than one hundred trillion connections are thought to exist within the human brain. Each connection can be compared to an individual microprocessor equipped with memory storage and information-processing abilities. In essence a single human brain has more connections than all the computer, router, and Internet interfaces in the entire world![9] If an idea is the result of all this computing power, why shouldn't we consider each and every one with some degree of seriousness? And if this kind of power exists behind every idea, why do we give up on our dreams so easily?

The creative mind encourages the development of new and innovative ideas. Instead of trying to limit the brain's potential through excuses, fears, doubts, and worries, the creative mind explores new possibilities freely without restraint empowering each of us not only to dream whatever we may desire but also to tap in to energies facilitating their realization. Did you know only 2 percent of the human brain is used during conscious activities? This means 98 percent of the activity of the human mind operates at a subconscious level. The human mind constantly receives inputs of which we are unaware. Associations, relationships, and connections are being contemplated constantly without any degree of conscious recognition. Our conscious thoughts emanate from a small fraction of our total brainpower, yet they have the ability either to foster idea creation or to shut off the potential to dream. The difference between a creative mind and a noncreative mind is simply the openness with which we consider each and every idea our minds may develop.

Let's assume for a moment that the human-resources director at one time dreamed of being the CEO of his own company. Perhaps he dreamed of creating weekend training curriculums for working adults who wished to start their own businesses. With his dream in mind, he started working for a corporation as a training director to gain some experience. After a few years, he was offered a promotion and a raise in salary. After a few more years, he was offered the directorship of the human-resources department. With each passing year, his dream to be his own boss was pushed further and further from his conscious thoughts. Ultimately he settled into his director position, lowering his expectations of success and allowing his dreams to lay dormant. Over several years he gradually allowed fear and doubt to creep into his mind about his abilities and about the feasibility of his dreams. Slowly his creative mind withered away from a lack of attention.

If we want to be successful, we need to appreciate the power of the creative mind. Not only does the creative mind provide endless potential to generate new ideas, but it also connects our ideas and dreams with the greater Creative Source, which permeates all existence. Through this connection with the Creative Source, the creative mind is infused with even greater abilities to conceive new ideas and possibilities. Each of us has unique talents and a destiny of success waiting for us to embrace it. In order to take the first step along this journey, all we need is to foster openness and positivity while resisting fear and doubt. In doing so we empower the creative mind to put forth ideas and dreams that will be sure to serve as the foundation of our wonderful success.

Nurturing Dreams and Idea Creation

We have all heard the saying "ideas are a dime a dozen." In actuality the statement is very true. When we were children, ideas ran rampant as our imaginations soared. As adults our ideas constantly stream into our consciousness whether we value them or not. Without question the mind is an active machine constantly feeding us with new considerations and thoughts.

While idea creation is important, even more significant is the ground upon which these ideas land. Do ideas enter your awareness and find open arms and intrigue, or do they meet immediate resistance and criticism? A key difference between those who succeed in life and those who don't resides in the mental garden encountered by potential dreams and ideas. Developing a creative mind is imperative for these seeds of success to grow and flourish.

Consider for a moment a situation where you were at your absolute best in terms of creating a solution to a problem. Were you filled with doubt about your abilities, or were you confident you would find some type of resolution? Did you invest a great deal of energy and willpower into finding an answer, or did you allow every roadblock to diminish your efforts? By far the best way to develop a creative mind and foster idea creation is to infuse your thoughts with positive energies. Positivity is an essential element of the creative mind and, as explained in the previous chapter, expands and broadens the mind, thus inviting a wider scope of ideas and possibilities to enter our conscious awareness. Determination and willpower are useful tools by which we force channels of thought open that would otherwise have been closed.

The positive energies of a creative mind also foster idea creation in another way. Think of the mind's capacity for creativity as a classroom in a school. Ideas and dreams originating in our subconscious minds represent the students who attend the school. As the students enter the classroom, they may choose to engage with each other, sharing their opinions and insights, or they may choose to keep their thoughts to themselves. What determines the choice they make? If the teacher is strict, strongly penalizes incorrect answers, and insists work be done a certain way, the student will probably refrain from freely volunteering information or expressing his or her ideas. On the other hand, if the teacher invites experimentation, gives consideration to alternative answers, and allows different learning strategies, the student will be more likely to share. The perceived environment of acceptance versus rejection affects whether or not the student will offer his or her own ideas to the group. Similarly our ability to encourage ideas and dreams within our minds is directly related to our attitude and perspective. Creative minds provide nurturing environments for ideas and dreams because they offer positive consideration and plenty of room to breathe.

If we meet an idea with doubt and resistance, then its ability to flourish into something wonderful is immediately restricted. If we allow fear to find fault with the idea because we can see success only through certain steps and efforts, innovative alternatives will never be found. More importantly, when we shut down these ideas with such a strict mental environment, over time they become less and less frequent. However, if we provide an open, positive, and accepting mindset in which ideas may be considered and valued, we increasingly give them power and facilitate a constant stream of new and wonderful creative considerations. The way we approach our dreams and ideas has a great deal to do with our ability to develop a truly creative mind.

Assuming we adopt positive thoughts and an inviting environment as a first step to nurturing our creative minds, ideas, and dreams requires additional attention to truly thrive. The seeds have found fertile soil, but sunlight and water must be provided for them to grow into seedlings and eventually robust plants. Similarly, ideas and dreams need nutrients to grow and flourish continually. Creative minds not only provide positive atmospheres for thoughts; they also provide two essential ingredients for success: belief and faith. The ability to believe in an idea completely and to have faith wholeheartedly in its eventual realization is incredibly powerful.

Over time I have met many wonderful people who always have pleasant attitudes, wear smiles on their faces, and appear to have the best outlooks on life. The weather may be gloomy outside, and life's pressures may be mounting, but these individuals seem always to focus on the bright side. Certainly their minds offer positive environments for ideas and dreams to develop, but in many instances these people never seem to attain the level of success they desire. Why? What is the difference between these individuals and those who attain their dreams? While other factors may also account for this, the lack of true belief and faith in their ideas and dreams often stands in their way. Ultimately this lack stems from where they choose to focus their attention.

Regardless of the external circumstances, these individuals insist on seeing the glass as half full, which is a wonderful perspective. But their shortcoming is a persistent focus on what's on the outside. They keep waiting day after day for their dreams to come true, hoping with the best intentions that something good will happen to them. In the process they give away all their power. They lose the ability to believe in themselves because they perceive outside circumstances are the main determinants of success. Belief and faith are internal empowerments. We energize ideas and dreams by knowing they will come true and having faith they will soon be reality. With this degree of belief and faith, willpower and determination follow. Instead of passively watching the seed and hoping it will grow, we take action, supplying it with all the nutrients it needs to truly flourish.

Months ago a close friend of mine experienced the rite of passage of having one of his children prepare to attend college. His daughter was extremely bright, and as a result she had been accepted to a rather prestigious and costly university. In every aspect his daughter is an exceptional individual. My friend, without hesitation, applied for a loan to support her college education.

As we began to go over the paperwork for the loan in my office, my friend expressed some concern. In essence he was betting it all on his daughter as the loan held all of his assets as collateral. He wanted to know my thoughts on the situation. I posed a single question to my friend: "Do you believe in your daughter?"

Immediately and emphatically my friend answered, "Yes!"

I replied, "Then you have absolutely nothing to be afraid of. When you believe in something so strongly that you are willing to bet it all, there is no way it can fail."

My friend had a dream his daughter would attend this university. He believed with all his heart she would excel as a result. He had faith his dream would become reality. And because of this faith, he was willing to put everything he owned on the line. When this degree of belief and faith are present, dreams cannot help but come true. The creative force behind such ideas is unstoppable when passions and energies provide such empowerment. Though my friend still had some fears due to the risk, his actions expressed the true depth of his faith.

The creative mind fosters idea creation and dream formation by opening the boundaries of thought and possibility. Openness and positivity create a fertile ground upon which ideas and dreams can be expressed and considered. Belief and faith then nurture these further, allowing them to grow in strength and power. Ultimately this leads to actions demonstrating our commitment to these ideas, and determination toward success follows. Every success, however, begins with a simple yet incredibly powerful thought. Ensuring each idea and dream has the room to breathe and grow is essential in attaining the success we desire. Of course this not only demands the right nutrients; it also requires identifying and eliminating factors hindering the development of a truly creative mind.

Safeguarding the Creative Mind

Developing a creative mind that encourages ideas and dreams is essential to success. Without ideas and dreams, success has no direction. The destination remains vague. Like a ship without a rudder, we let the turbulent waters of life push us around without any type of guiding force. Unfortunately many people find themselves in such a situation because they have given up on their dreams or no longer give their ideas any degree of power. As children we all enjoyed creative minds that allowed for wonderful imaginations. But as we grew older, we had to safeguard this ability to allow new ideas and far-reaching dreams to continue to occupy our thoughts. All too often we let experience and other influences slowly take away our minds' creative potential.

What is the largest dream you have for yourself?

What truly defines success for you?

For many people the answer might be "to be wealthy" or "to be famous." These responses are not really dreams, however, at least not in the sense needed to guide success. The creative mind does not stop at such limited visions or descriptions. Instead the creative mind consumes our thoughts and mental images with exquisite details, showing us vividly—and often precisely—what our dreams should be. Imagine I am planning a trip. When asked my destination, I simply reply, "Europe." I might end up in Venice, Italy, or Berat, Albania. The first step in safeguarding our ability to dream and to create new ideas is to be specific and allow our minds to fill in the details of our utmost desires. The creative mind enjoys spending time thinking about all the possibilities and relishes these subtle nuances.

How many times do you squash an idea before it even has a chance to set up shop? A friend of mind loves talking about potential business concepts. But despite having literally hundreds of ideas, she has never actually acted upon any of them. The last idea involved recreating celebrity-style weddings for the masses at affordable prices. But before the idea even had a chance to breathe, she had already itemized a list of reasons why such a business would fail. It's like a lawnmower that will never start because the owner refuses to take the choke off the carburetor. Unfortunately many of us are guilty of this habit. Unless we can see the path, we immediately discount the possibility of the idea.

Human nature often insists we know the "how" before we can believe in the result. Unfortunately this approach is completely backward. The creative mind does not provide us all the steps in advance so we may have greater faith in an idea. In all likelihood our conscious mind would be unable to grasp all the details of such information anyway. Instead the creative mind provides us with the dream, and, by our having faith and belief in its realization, the process by which it comes true is slowly revealed.

A word of caution is needed here, however. Simply believing in a dream and the end result is not enough for its realization. Planning and action are still needed. However, we do not need to know all the tasks involved to order to have belief in the eventual outcome. The actual power comes from the creative idea itself combined with belief, faith, and action. When we insist on defining all the steps involved, we allow doubt to appear. When this occurs the power of the creative mind slowly diminishes.

Doubt can immediately reduce the capacity of the creative mind to develop ideas and expand dreams. However, with perpetual doubt even the formation of ideas and dreams can become affected. Questions and concerns often come from self-doubt, but uncertainty can also arise from sources outside of us. Among the most common sources of doubt are our friends and families. Instead of lending support and encouragement, those close to us can actually hinder our minds' creativity as they find reasons for our ideas and dreams to falter. This concept may seem ridiculous, but these negative influences are not purposeful actions to cause us to fail. In actuality these hindrances usually have good intentions.

Family members and friends naturally have our best interests at heart. But as we offer our own dreams and ideas for consideration, the tendency to criticize and find fault stems from a desire to protect. By identifying possible shortcomings, they might prevent us from failure or pain. They instill fear and doubt out of a sense of love and loyalty. However, their perspectives are short-sighted. Little do they realize they are encouraging us to limit our potential when they question our dreams. By giving power to the doubts and fears of friends and family members, we constrain our minds and inhibit creativity. Often such fears are passed down from generation to generation, no different from other family traditions. If your family has a tradition of doubt, this is one part of your heritage you will want to let go.

In addition to interactions with friends and family members, life experiences offer more potential threats to the creative mind. Failures can be painful, embarrassing, and humiliating. Setbacks can be irritating and disheartening. When these circumstances occur, we often retract our minds' creativity and play it assumedly safe. By corralling our dreams, we incorrectly presume we are taking less risk. But in reality nothing could be more false. By restricting our own abilities to dream and create new ideas, we naturally place greater trust in external circumstances or in other people. Nothing could be riskier than this! Each of us is unique, and our creative minds allow us to explore that uniqueness in all its glory. Though we believe we are protecting ourselves from future hurts by downplaying our dreams and desires, in reality we are only relinquishing our ability to succeed.

As will be discussed in other chapters, setbacks and obstacles are not experiences to be feared or events that should prevent further creative exploration. In fact these seemingly unfortunate experiences are often blessings in disguise. In many instances they offer keen insights and revelations that empower creativity to even greater heights. Instead of being perceived as sources of discomfort, see them as opportunities in which new ideas are needed in order to overcome and persevere. With every negative circumstance, we have a choice. We can either retract or suppress our ability to dream, or we can seize the moment and expand our creative minds to even greater heights. The road to success follows the latter path.

Doubts and fears are like weeds in the garden. In a creative mind, the soil is rich. Ingredients for nourishment are readily available. As a result ideas and dreams grow and multiply. But when doubts and fears begin to enter, slowly nutrients are depleted, and ideas and dreams become choked. These weeds may enter through self-doubt, or they may be introduced through people we respect. And sometimes they develop in response to unfortunate circumstances and experiences we have encountered along the way. In order to safeguard the garden of the creative mind so ideas and dreams can foster our success, awareness of these risks is essential. Fortunately practical exercises and routines can be employed to help develop and maintain a creative mind. Because ideas and dreams are the cornerstones of success, we must invest energy and effort into always developing a creative mindset.

Strategies for Dreaming and Idea Creation

No matter how constrained your mind has become through self-doubt, negative experiences, and the cautions of others, regaining a creative mindset and fostering the ability to dream and create imaginative ideas is easily achieved. Several strategies and exercises can be performed to expand the boundaries of the mind and energize new ideas with possibility. We must realize that ideas have a creative force like few things in life. Despite our inability to see them, ideas and dreams are the true drivers of success. If we respect this fact and invest our efforts in developing a creative mind capable of transforming these ideas and dreams into reality, we can attain any goal in which we truly believe.

- *Creative Escapes*
  (one hour weekly)
  It's no wonder that as adults we have difficulty embracing a creative mind. We are constantly being stimulated by messages promoting paranoia, worry,

and fear. It becomes much easier to complain than it does to express gratitude. Despite the advancement of technological efficiencies, we find we have less and less time to reflect and ponder. Each of these things constrains our minds and usurps energy away from our creativity. Instead of having a perspective of open-ness and wonder, we drain every possible idea of its power as we list the reasons why it is destined to fail or lead to some unforeseen negative outcome. This is no environment for dreams of success.

Once a week we need to allow our minds the pleasure of expansion and openness. Set aside a time when you can explore something completely fresh and new without any expectations whatsoever. Do not assign the activity any particular objective or goal, but make sure the experience carries a sense of positive anticipation. Some examples might be an hour at an art museum, a walk along a waterfront park, or even participating in a community project. Just like our physical bodies, the creative mind enjoys variety and new tastes. New ideas and desires evolve from such experiences, and our ability to dream is enhanced through the process.

- ***Journaling***
  (fifteen minutes daily)
  I have several different journals that allow me to maintain a creative mindset. I have a gratitude journal where I express those things for which I am most appreciative. I have a reflection journal where I reflect on past ideas, dreams, and goals and their realizations within my life. I have an idea journal where I simply

allow my mind to express itself as free thought moving in any direction it likes without any guidance whatsoever. Over the years the degree of liberation this has provided my thoughts and dreams has been well beyond anything I could have anticipated. Repeatedly new ideas and connections that never would have occurred otherwise appear as a result of this activity.

While free thought is a central component of journaling, enabling constraints to be removed, and a nurturing environment in which the creative mind can explore possibilities, I do routinely include a wish list in my journals that expressly documents my greatest dreams and visions. As we will discuss in the chapter covering vision boards, these written expressions carry great power in transforming ideas and dreams into reality. Within our subconscious mind, these written words are recorded and stored away. Though we are unaware of it, simply writing these statements down demonstrates a degree of belief and faith that helps make our dreams come true.

- *Brainstorming*
  (ten minutes every morning)
  Brainstorming is a great activity to stimulate creative ideas. I personally choose to brainstorm every morning, when I allot several minutes to challenge my brain about an upcoming dilemma, project, or new endeavor. For example I might be considering whether or not to purchase an existing business. I would begin the brainstorming process by asking myself a question like, "How can I make this business better?" The answer might include a list of possible

options, each of which I prioritize and consider. I might then ask, "How can this idea further other projects I am pursuing?" Through the process of questioning myself and insisting on answers, I am encouraging idea creation. I am fueling my mind with the energy that is being used to create new ideas and consider a variety of possibilities.

Brainstorming is to the creative mind as weight-lifting is to one's muscles. With routine exercise and a desire to become stronger, the ability to generate ideas and dreams improves day after day, week after week. The process of questioning and answering forces the mind to consider new options and to think outside the box. After you have been performing this exercise regularly for a time, you will begin to see your ideas come to life. These experiences, unlike negative experiences, provide positive feedback that strengthens your commitment to your brainstorming routine.

• *Seeds for Sleep*
  (five minutes before sleep)
  Tapping in to the subconscious mind offers great opportunities to explore our brains' creative potential. In addition the connection between our creative mind and the pervasive Creative Force likely occurs to a great extent at a subconscious level. Sleep represents a state of consciousness that enables our subconscious mind to take over our thoughts without interference of the conscious mind. When we "sleep on it," we truly turn over a problem to our subconscious mind and its creative abilities. By planting seeds of inquiry just

before slumber, we encourage our subconscious to explore new ideas and considerations.

Every night before I go to sleep, I consider three or more questions for which I would like answers. Rather than consciously dwelling on them (and possibly suffering from insomnia), I simply acknowledge the questions and write them down, and then I turn off the lights and go to sleep. Though I am asleep, my subconscious brain is still quite active, as science has repeatedly demonstrated. I keep a notebook at my bedside in which I can record any revelations if an idea awakens me in the night. Many times I awaken with a completely new perspective on the dilemma. Plant these seeds before you sleep, and you also will be amazed at the creative results.

These activities provide the tools by which we can develop a more creative mindset that in turn fosters the mind's ability to consider new ideas and to dream in ways never before realized. No idea is too far-fetched, and no dream is too big. Reach for the stars. Set your expectations high. The creative mind has no limits and is most powerful when constraints and boundaries are removed. By acknowledging ideas and dreams as the essential foundations of all our future successes, we must naturally pursue activities to strengthen our minds' ability to think creatively and expansively. Once this is in place, absolutely nothing can keep you from attaining all of your heart's (and mind's) desires.

Chapter Three

Envisioning Your Dreams: Seeing Is Believing

Among my many passions, I have a love of fine automobiles. For as long as I can remember, my favorite car was a Ferrari Modena Spider, and I dreamt of having one at some point in my life. In 2008 I was in no position to consider such a luxury, but that did not stop me from dreaming about it. Not only did I dream about the exact image of the car, but my visions were in vivid color with exquisite detail. The car of my dreams boasted a brilliantly warm shade of yellow with rich, black leather interior and dazzling chrome wheels. And despite my less than wealthy status, I located the exact car nearby in Naples, Florida. For years after this, I kept a picture of it and referred to it often. Though my dream was visually tangible, I did not have the means to make it reality...at least not at that particular moment.

Fast forward to 2012. Through my development of a creative mind, my life had transformed dramatically. Hopes of success were becoming realities, and I was now in a position to pursue the car of my dreams. Unfortunately the exact Ferrari I had envisioned was nowhere to be found. After searching and searching, I finally found in California the color and style of Modena Spider I previously desired. After some deliberation I bit the bullet and ordered the car to be shipped from the West Coast to Florida. But on receiving the car, I found something was eerily familiar about it. It looked exactly like the one in the picture I had kept all those years. Interestingly enough I contacted the dealer in California, and they informed me they had recently purchased the car elsewhere...in Naples!

Envisioning our dreams is a powerful tool for realizing success few people recognize. Something amazing happens when the creative mind focuses on a specific image and that image is infused with passion, desire, and faith. Despite initially lacking the ability to buy the Ferrari, and despite a lack of understanding of how I would ever attain the means, I knew deep down I would have that car one day. And while passion, desire, and faith are incredibly important ingredients, capturing a visual image detailing my dream carried a great force in converting it to reality. In this chapter we will explore why envisioning dreams within the creative mind is critically important along our journey toward success.

How Visualizations Guide Success

Many of us are visual by nature. The popularity of television, theater, cinema, YouTube videos, and more demonstrates our preference to see and watch. After all a picture is truly worth a thousand words, and visual images provide a rich context in many ways.

In considering the anatomy of the brain, this tendency to prefer visual over other types of sensory input makes perfect sense. Large portions of the human brain are dedicated to visual imagery. Images we see travel from our eyes' retinas all the way to large areas of cortex in the back of the brain, and along the way numerous connections are made with other sensory areas, emotional areas, and memory circuits. Compared to touch, taste, smell, and hearing, visual stimulations have a much more pronounced effect on our overall perceptions, memories, and experiences.

Of course we do not routinely appreciate the impact visualizations have on us. Scientists estimate that as human beings we utilize only approximately 2 percent of our brains for conscious activities. The remaining 98 percent operates at a subconscious level. Therefore the power of visualizations likely occurs at a subliminal level within the mind, exerting a force we cannot perceive. While I consciously knew I wanted the Ferrari and established a goal to pursue it, I was not aware the car I was purchasing was the exact car I had visualized for years and years. Deep within my creative mind, the repeated visualizations of the exact Ferrari about which I had dreamt guided my actions as well as other circumstances in the universe to make this come true. While the "how" of this incredible phenomenon remains an enigma, the results are amazing nonetheless.

What if each of us visualized with precision the life we wished to lead? Perhaps our dream lives would include prestigious careers, wealth, and status, or we might desire the ability to contribute generously to the world in the form of charity and humanitarian efforts. But simply envisioning an image is not enough. Like the ideas and dreams discussed in the last chapter, visualizations must be infused with the psychic energies of the creative mind to transform image into reality. Such psychic energies include passion, desire, belief, and faith, and visualizations require taking actions to transform them into reality. I might have a photograph of a deep-sea fishing boat as my computer screensaver, but unless I have a desire for that boat and pursue actions to acquire it through belief and faith, that image will carry little force.

From this perspective visualizations are tangible manifestations of our ideas and dreams. If the images are developed with a creative mind and are immersed in positive thought, strong beliefs, and unwavering faith, they have remarkable effects on our lives. But if we simply stare at an image and hope life will hand deliver it to us at some point, the transforming power of visualizations is lost. Success demands active engagement on our parts. We invite engagement when we exercise creativity and positivity, and we actively engage when we plan and pursue goals according to our belief and faith. Visualizations are simply additional tools by which we can enhance our creative minds to develop the success we truly desire. And because the human brain loves visual images, this instrument can be incredibly powerful.

Because the effect of visualizations in transforming dreams into success occurs at a subconscious level, we should learn to value our instincts. For example if we see an image we find appealing but do not understand its significance in our lives, this phenomenon could very well be our subconscious mind communicating with us. We see this effect with suppressed memories on occasion. From a negative perspective, soldiers returning from combat suffering from post-traumatic stress disorder often experience visual flashbacks. Many of these images carry powerful scenes recorded by the subconscious mind but suppressed by the conscious awareness. Similarly the image of a particular scene may provide immediate comfort despite the individual's never actually having enjoyed such an experience in the past.

In such situations instinctually we may feel drawn to some visualizations and wish to push away from others. This likely emanates from the subconscious aspects of our creative minds. In fact these gut reactions may involve more-significant connections with other universal energies through the law of attraction. For example images filled with positive energies may lure us toward them when we embrace our creative minds and positivity. Such instincts may also involve a more-powerful connection to the Creative Source that exists in all of life. Regardless of how the subconscious gets our attention through visual imagery, the fact remains that the human mind is strongly affected by visual stimulation and visual images. Because of this, visualizing dreams and ideas can serve to further their transformation into reality and pave the way toward great success.

Vision Boards and Visualizations

Remember creating a collage of images on a picture board when you were a teenager or child? Perhaps you cut and pasted images of friends, events, clothes, sports stars, or a host of other things. In essence you were creating a vision board. Increasingly I realize we previously harbored impressive creative energies as children, thus showcasing our possession then of a truly creative mind. We were open to ideas without fear or doubt. We dared to dream of the most spectacular possibilities for our lives, and we invested a great deal of passion and energy into visualizing these dreams. A collage or vision board was just one of the ways we demonstrated our belief and faith that our dreams were indeed going to happen. Therefore returning to a childhood perspective of imagination, dreaming, and visualization is important in developing our creative minds. Vision boards offer an easy yet excellent way to recapture this ability.

I regularly make trips to my local bookstore and select a variety of magazines that appeal to me. Some might be car magazines; others might have to do with entertainment or business. I let my imagination go wild as I gaze at the magazine rack, allowing my creative mind to explore any possibility through the colorful images. Not only is this exercise a creative escape for my brain, but what my mind finds exciting constantly surprises me. After selecting an array of magazines, I purchase them and proceed to create my own collage of images on a common poster board. And once it's complete, I position my vision board in a spot where I will notice it frequently throughout the day.

In creating a vision board, keeping an open mind is important. As I walk into the bookstore, I harbor no preconceived notions of what images might appeal to me. In other words I simply let my instincts and subconscious mind participate in selecting which pictures and photographs are interesting, intriguing, or exciting. Many images have obvious relationships with my goals of success, but in some instances the connection between my interest in the image and my known life objectives is puzzling. These situations often lead to some of the most amazing circumstances.

Recently I was updating my vision board, which I do every few weeks. As I perused various magazines, I saw an image of the "sharks" from the television program *Shark Tank*. While I enjoy the program immensely, the photograph had no particular meaning to me in relation to my own success goals. Regardless, I could not help being attracted to the picture. Ultimately I listened to my creative mind and bought the magazine, and subsequently placed the picture of the sharks on my vision board. Even though I could not understand its significance, something within encouraged me to include this among my other visualizations.

Over the next few weeks, I was actively involved in negotiations with a network concerning my participation in some co-marketing activities. Despite our seemingly coming close to an agreement, the network suddenly began dragging its feet and introducing additional questions and concerns. Every time I thought we had finalized the terms, another delay would appear. Amid these delays my marketing and production colleague called me one day with some interesting news. Daymond Johnson was visiting Miami and had spoken with my colleague. This gentleman had expressed an interest in providing me with an opportunity to co-market with him. By the way Daymond Johnson happens to be one of the "sharks" on *Shark Tank* and the current CEO of FUBU.

This collaboration with Daymond Johnson as well as with some of the other sharks continues to evolve in very positive ways, and the importance of listening to one's instincts cannot be stressed enough. I had no idea how the sharks from *Shark Tank* might relate to my visions of success. But subconsciously, and perhaps through the larger Creative Force, the image of these television personalities aroused interest and excitement within me. And because I acted on faith that this instinct was important despite not knowing all the details, the visualization was awarded greater power. Day after day I would see the picture of the sharks on my vision board, and its significance became apparent within a couple of months. A tour entitled "Shark Tour 2013 Business Expo and Career Fair," presented by me, is now scheduled to open in Orlando, Florida, in November 2013. This became a reality because of my openness to consider the seemingly impossible and the power of this image on my vision board. Like ideas and dreams, visualizations become incredibly powerful when energized with faith and belief.

In addition to my actual vision board, I routinely take photographs of my vision board and place them in various locations where I am sure to see them. I have saved my vision board both on my computer desktop and as wallpaper on my smartphone. I have even pasted the photograph at the top of my daily work list at times. In addition I add and update my visual board often. As some of my vision board images become reality, I save them for the purpose of reflection and replace them with new visual images. Not only does this allow my vision board to be current, but it also constantly stimulates the creative mind to explore new images and possibilities. Over time, I have found, this exercise alone is an excellent way to foster greater creativity and imagination.

Vision boards have become an integral part of my creative process and essential in turning ideas and dreams into reality. While creative thoughts are intangible, making them tangible by creating a vision board facilitates belief. Just as writing down objectives and life goals help keep you accountable to your dreams, vision boards accomplish this while also enhancing the ability to assign positive emotions and desire to the images. Seeing a picture of something you desire naturally evokes strong emotions, and this energy helps transform a dream into reality.

Goals and Deadlines—Giving Power to the Visions

Often people will appreciate my current successes and assume I naturally enjoyed a nurturing environment as a child. Many individuals assume some favored advantage when they witness a person's success for the first time. Perhaps because they have not yet attained success, this assumption provides them with a sense of comfort—and an excuse for their lack of success since they did not have these presumed advantages. How often have you heard someone claim it takes money to make money? This belief aligns with this type of assumption. Unfortunately many people live their entire lives never realizing success was at their fingertips as well. All they needed to do was to foster a creative mind and believe in their own abilities.

My childhood certainly offered few advantages in terms of my environment. I grew up in a less-than-attractive part of Brooklyn; my mother raised my sisters and me with the aid of part-time jobs and government assistance. At the age eight, I had my first business shoveling snow for the neighbors, and by fourteen I was working at McDonald's. Even then I dreamt of succeeding in life, and I struggled to understand why some restaurant managers, who were well into middle age, lacked any vision to grow and advance their levels of success. There's absolutely nothing wrong with such a position, but these men and women lacked desire, passion, and the ability to dream. From their actions and words, their resignation from even pursuing success was evident.

What I lacked in money and opportunity, I compensated for in passion and determination. No one in my immediate family had ever finished college, but I was determined to complete my education and attain a law degree. In fact my goal was not simply to achieve these accomplishments but to do so within record time. I planned to complete college within three years and law school within two and a half...and I did just that. Not only did I visualize my success in education, I established a goal and stuck to it. As a result my vision became reality. During that time I realized visualizations provide incredible power toward generating success. Though they cannot materialize success in isolation, visualizations are important tools to help us along our journey.

Perhaps my managers at McDonald's had simply failed to act on their original visions. Maybe they dreamed of owning one or more McDonald's franchises in time. They even might have envisioned the personal benefits this would provide. But if they failed to establish this aspiration as a goal and take specific actions toward it, the vision slowly lost power and withered away. Their situations could change even now if they simply reenergized their visions with passion and action. It's never too late to reclaim your creative mind and to fulfill your potential destiny. But it does take more than visual images.

Throughout the ages a debate over fate versus freewill has existed. Some believe fate controls one's destiny while others believe freewill determines the degree of success one experiences. But what if both apply? Similar arguments over nature versus nurture have been ongoing, but science is now demonstrating how our own DNA changes in relation to the immediate environment[10]. In other words both nature and nurture are important. By the same rationale, fate and freewill can indeed coexist. Fate determines our potential destiny; freewill determines whether or not we realize it. Destiny thus requires effort on our parts.

Each of us has unique potential. Our individual destinies are specific to who we are. Why do some people become excited and passionate about creating new inventions while others are fueled by athletic achievement? Why do some individuals demonstrate incredible technical intelligence and others show extreme skills in visual arts? Our uniqueness reflects our potential destiny, and when we dream and visualize our dreams we are allowing our creative mind to express that destiny. The only thing preventing us from actually realizing our ultimate fate is our ability to believe in our visions and act upon them in faith. Fate gets us started along the path, but freewill opens the gates.

So how do we energize our visualizations? How can we embrace our destiny and take action accordingly? The short answer is through establishing goals, deadlines, and metrics. To use a common analogy, the absence of goals is like a ship sailing without any known destination. The absence of deadlines for attaining our goals means the ship could take an eternity to arrive at its port. And the absence of metrics along the way to assess progress is similar to navigating without a compass. Goals, deadlines, and metrics are the essential tools needed to make visualizations come to life. These aspects of planning and action fuel our visions with belief because when we act, we are exhibiting proof that we believe our time and energy are not being wasted. And at the same time, we are holding ourselves accountable as active participants in achieving success. In other words we aren't sitting back waiting for fate to appear. When we indulge in visualizations of our dreams and desires, we begin to appreciate all the success we can have in life. When we plan steps toward goals that will achieve these visualizations, we use positive energies to enhance the creative mind. When we then act on these plans and hold ourselves accountable in time, we set in motion a chain of events attracting people and events toward us that enable these visualizations to become real. Though obstacles may come, belief demonstrated in both thought and action nurtures patience and determination. Through it all, remaining focused on the visions that reflect our unique desires and destiny strengthens our will and ultimately brings success.

I wholeheartedly believed in my dream of completing college in three years. Though I did not have a vision board at the time, I envisioned myself dressed in a cap and gown while accepting my bachelor's degree. I realized also that accelerating my coursework would require significant effort on my part. As I began to consider turning my visions into reality, I studied the steps required and the timelines needed in order to attain my degree in an abbreviated time. From these I established goals and deadlines and developed metrics along the way to be sure I was on pace. If I fell behind, I immediately realized it and took efforts to stay on track.

Goals, deadlines, and metrics are tools that help us maintain a hunger for our success. If we achieve a short-term goal, we become more confident in our abilities and more dedicated to the cause. And if we fail to meet a goal, we are reminded that we must persevere and use the challenge as a learning experience. Planning actions to attain a dream and holding ourselves accountable for their accomplishment keeps us hungry for success. Deadlines simultaneously keep us on edge and give us an edge as well. If we truly believe in our visions and dreams and actively pursue a plan to attain them, we avoid becoming complacent, distracted, or resigned.

My friends know some of my favorite movies include the series of Rocky films. In addition to being inspirational, they contain many small pearls of wisdom. One scene in particular demonstrating the need to stay focused and passionate about success came in *Rocky III*, when Mickey, Rocky's coach, said, "The worst thing that happened to you, that can happen to any fighter. You got civilized."[11] There Rocky stood in his $2,000 suit looking dumbfounded, but, as was usually the case, Mickey spoke the truth. Rocky had become complacent with his current level of success. He had lost his hunger and had lost track of his vision. Without goals, deadlines, and metrics, we tend to lose our hunger. These ingredients are important to continually fuel our visions with power, energy, and passion. These ingredients hold us accountable to our potential destiny and foster the determination to keep on striving toward the success we deserve.

Practical Strategies for Envisioning Success

Some people need little assistance when it comes to envisioning success. Images of wealth, status, and fame can be readily created within the mind's eye for most individuals. However, the challenge is to envision *your* success, not some generic, Hollywood-based version of accomplishment. Only you know your specific talents, desires, passions, and dreams. Only you can assign specific details to these visualizations that speak directly to your spirit and soul. The more specific our visualizations, the more passion we have for them. And the more passion we have, the greater will be our determination in making them a reality.

- ***Create and Maintain a Vision Board***
  (sixty minutes monthly)
  As is evident from our discussion of visions boards, creating your own vision board with your own visualizations, images, and pictures is critical when making your dreams and desires more tangible. And the process of creating your vision board should be enjoyable, inspiring, and motivating. Take the time to select images that precisely capture exactly what you aspire to become, have, or enjoy. The more detailed your visualizations, the more your vision board will speak to your conscious and subconscious mind. The time you take to create your vision board should thus be a period of reflection and creativity.

  I update my vision board often. Most commonly this is accomplished simply by adding and changing out pictures on my board. For this reason some people prefer a bulletin board due to the ease of removing old images and adding new ones. Others simply replace their entire vision board with new images because the process of creating the vision board itself fuels their creative mind. Either way, vision boards should be regularly updated since our lives are always changing, advancing, and progressing. As we achieve some dreams, new ones will appear. After all the desire of all of life is to grow and advance. Your vision board should reflect this ever-changing pursuit of greater success.

- ***Spread the Wealth (of Visualizations)***
  (five minutes daily)
  Placing your vision board in a location where you will frequently see your visualized dreams is imperative.

The more often your chosen images are seen, studied, and contemplated, the more engrained these visualizations will become in your conscious and subconscious pursuits. In this age of digitalized technology, the ability to enhance the visibility of your vision board is easy. My process involves taking a digital photograph of my vision board each time it is updated. I will then place the photo on my smartphone, computer screen, music device, and more. As a result my vision board "speaks" to me multiple times throughout the day in a variety of situations.

Many develop creative ways of enhancing this exercise. For example you could schedule an e-mail to be sent to yourself that includes a photograph of your vision board. Or perhaps you can add a degree of accountability to this exercise by sharing your vision board with a select few individuals who will ask about your progress from time to time. The key is to ensure you have a vision board that is not only living and current but also readily seen. The creative mind has different revelations when environments change. By visually spreading the number of contexts in which your vision board is viewed, you continually invest in greater opportunities for success.

- *Visually Inspiring Your Creative Mind*
  (ten minutes weekly to sixty minutes monthly)
  The creative mind is a visual mind. The more opportunities to see pictures of what our dreams and desires look like, the more likely it is they will become reality. Imagine trying to become a culinary expert by eating unseasoned baked chicken and steamed vegetables at

every meal. Perhaps you'd be rather healthy, but your ability to appreciate exotic tastes would be quite poor. In order for us to develop detailed vision boards that capture who we are and what we wish to attain, we must visually stimulate our minds with an array of images. The more this occurs, the more accurate our vision board will become.

I find the magazine rack at a large bookstore ideal for visually stimulating my mind, but plenty of other opportunities exist. Art events, window shopping, and perhaps test driving you dream car all may enhance your innate visualizations of your desires. At the same time, such activities offer innovative escapes to help foster creativity. You should ultimately pursue whatever you believe best encourages more accurate images of your dreams. Provide your creative mind with the visual nourishment it needs to truly envision the success you desire.

- ### *Reflect on Past Visualizations*
  (five minutes weekly to thirty minutes monthly)
  In order to appreciate where you are going, you must understand where you have been. All of us have roots and foundations of our pasts that influence our perspectives of the world and of life. In striving to realize our future successes and achieve our potential destiny, revisiting past accomplishments can serve as empowering opportunities that add to our inspiration and motivation. Because of this, revisiting old vision boards from months and years prior can be incredibly revealing. Because we focus on current goals and pursuits, we often forget past successes. But these can be

the best pieces of evidence demonstrating the power of the creative mind.

Perusing past vision boards can be done digitally on your computer or smartphone while waiting for an appointment or while taking a brief mental break. Or you can use this activity as a creative escape where you reflect more deeply on a past visualization and how it resulted in important life changes. This exercise may even reveal new insights and revelations about how to pursue current goals and dreams. Whether its used for building confidence and support or as a means to expand your creative abilities, revisiting past vision boards can be a very useful exercise.

As we develop a more creative mind, the ability to envision success comes easier with practice. In addition, as visualizations repeatedly come true and we replace them with new ones, our strength of belief and faith grows, encouraging us to dream bigger and adopt more grandiose visualizations. Once we realize we can attain any vision we want through a creative mind, we finally loosen the shackles and expand our abilities to see our dreams through images. The creative mind can even reach the point where it becomes instinctively attracted to some images without consciously knowing why. Developing the ability to envision our dreams and success is thus an important tool of the creative mind in our pursuit of success.

Chapter Four

Preparing for Success: Mind, Body, and Spirit

At this point we have considered the foundations of success, which involve developing the creative mind. By inviting positive thinking and idea creation combined with dreams and their associated visualizations, we establish the groundwork for success and the realization of our destiny. However, many people stop here. The dreamer is adept at dreaming but fails to put together a plan. And we shoot down many ideas before they even have a chance. In order to reach the level of success we desire, we have to act upon these creative resources. This ability to act, however, demands more than simple, rudimentary effort. We must prepare ourselves thoroughly for the challenges ahead.

But how do we prepare in order to overcome the certain struggles and obstacles we will experience? This chapter will explore all the facets of this very question. Success demands we attend to the preparation of ourselves in a holistic manner. Consider the intellectual who has acquired tremendous knowledge within a field of study but lacks the creativity to apply this knowledge in practical ways. Or consider the talented athlete who has climbed through scholastic and collegiate levels only to fall short of a professional career due to an inability to grasp the playbook. Success requires an open, creative perspective on life. The creative mind does not compartmentalize ideas and dreams but instead encourages interrelations and interconnectivity. In the same way, we must allow our mind, body, and spirit to interconnect, enabling new visions and revelations.

Dedicated preparation to success thus involves time spent on developing our intellect, our physical health, and our spiritual strength. The interrelation of these efforts becomes increasingly evident the more we invest in their development. A healthy body relieves stress while building confidence. A prepared mind perceives creative opportunities more readily. And a strong spirit fosters creativity, belief, and faith. Each strengthens our ability to attain success. Preparing each of these areas therefore becomes important in enhancing determination and perseverance and in our ability to transform dreams into reality.

Preparation of the Mind

When we think of preparing one's mind, we naturally think about education and the acquisition of knowledge. Most people believe true mental preparation thus comes from formal schooling— high school, college, graduate school, and training. While these opportunities for learning are important, numerous success stories have involved individuals without any formal education whatsoever.[12] Consider the owner of the landscape company who manages my home's lawn care. Like many of his employees, he has a high school degree. But unlike his employees, he enjoys owning a business worth hundreds of thousands of dollars. In fact his own home is comparable to most of the ones he services. Was he just lucky, or does some other answer lie beneath his success?

In all likelihood the landscaper enjoys a natural passion for his profession. From firsthand experience I know he demonstrates interest and enthusiasm in designing and caring for plants and in creating aesthetically pleasing landscapes. But passion only gets you to the door and encourages you to knock. One of the means by which the landscaper excelled was self-study and experiential learning. He may not have received a college degree in biology and horticulture, but his knowledge of landscaping is superior to every other landscaper I have known. His success resulted not from luck or circumstance but from dedicated preparation of his mind in an industry he loved. In other words he studied about his passions and was passionate about his studies.

The first step in preparing our minds for success thus involves defining our own passions. For some of us, this task may be simple. But for others, particularly those who may have suppressed their creative minds over time, finding true passions may take some effort. For those confused about what ignites their interests and desires, paying attention to emotions during daily activities can be revealing. What activity are you doing when you lose track of time? When do you feel true excitement? Which activities do you look forward to doing? Answers to these questions and the subsequent "why" questions can help lead you in identifying inner passions and desires. Once this is accomplished, preparing your mind becomes much more straightforward.

No matter what dream is being pursued, preparation of the mind involves completely and thoroughly knowing your field. If you wish to become successful in providing children's entertainment, then study concerning current child entertainment offerings, competitors, customer demands, industry secrets, and much more should be explored. Through the use of libraries, bookstores, the Internet, and journals, much can be learned outside of formal schools, providing keen insights and knowledge. Likewise social connections, public lectures, and an inquisitive nature can further one's intellect about a particular industry. Within a short time, the same information begins to reappear concerning a subject of interest, indicating a solid working knowledge of the field.

Preparing the mind for success involves more than knowledge acquisition, however. After all success develops from a creative mind, not just a knowledgeable mind. From this viewpoint one must also encourage an open, creative perspective when acquiring knowledge and insights. For example suppose I am offered the chance to buy one of two businesses. The first business enjoys annual profits, good stability, and a solid customer base. The second business is struggling, has infrastructure problems, and is disorganized in its process management. Many would never consider the second company for purchase, but the second business instantly has greater interest and appeal to me. Why? Because the opportunity to enhance value through creativity in the second business is much greater. While this would not be the only issue to be explored, on the surface it seems as though developing and implementing new ideas within the second business offers greater potential for success and, ultimately, more profit than the first business. This is especially true when the purchase price of the second business is markedly less due to its being a poorly performing asset.

The creative mind views everything as having room for improvement. Exploring new angles, new markets, and new products and services offers a chance for growth and progress. Being knowledgeable and learning as much as possible about a subject remains a core ingredient of preparing the mind, but simultaneously we must pursue creative preparations as we investigate all the existing potential. We must study not only an industry of interest but potential pathways toward success as well. In other words what proven methods of attaining success have been revealed? Research and study provide the mind with practical tools while creativity and positive thinking direct the use of these tools in innovative and imaginative ways. When both exist, success becomes more readily attained because we now approach every situation with a well-prepared creative mind. Even after a level of success is reached, the task of preparing one's mind continues to be necessary. For one, change is constant, and business environments, regulatory demands, consumer wants, technology, and a host of other areas require us to continually prepare our minds intellectually and creatively. In addition everything in life has an innate drive to grow and advance. This simple fact supports the notion that success is attainable by everyone. If success were not a ubiquitous opportunity, this inner drive to attain more in life would not exist. Therefore we must always prepare our minds for change and for the next chance of success lying around the corner.

Preparation of the Body

When we think about the road to success, preparation of the mind is readily accepted as a necessary task. After all we are rational beings who have advanced society throughout the ages with intellectual discoveries. But few of us appreciate the importance of preparing our bodies for success as well. We should not perceive our mental health as being separate and distinct from our physical health (or spiritual health for that matter). A shift in Westernized medicine over the last few decades has brought us to realize this fact as well. Scientific and medical discoveries are demonstrating the powerful effects of positive thought over physical health and vice versa.[13] Therefore, taking care of our bodies becomes an equally important task in planning for success.

This revelation came to me at one of the lowest points in my life. I might say one of the worst, but, as I later realized, obstacles are usually blessings in disguise. Having been terminated a few weeks prior from the law firm at which I worked due to a serious difference in personal philosophies, I sat alone in my car staring at the windshield. In a short time, I had blown through what little savings I had, leaving me with $37 on a credit card. I had secured a tiny law office not more than one hundred square feet in size. And emotionally I was drained. Amid all the fears, worries, and dejection, I found myself with a choice among a few limited options. I could apply for unemployment, which I refused to do out of pride. I could search for another law position with another firm and settle for what I could get. Or I could risk everything in an effort to pursue my own dreams of success. Fortunately I chose the latter.

The next morning and every morning after that, I started my day at the gym. For months I had neglected my physical health, being consumed with the routine demands of the day. But with newfound determination, I channeled my energies not only into developing creative concepts for work but also into regaining my physical strength and endurance. The more fit I felt, the more confident I became. Just I progressively achieved my goals in my workout routine, my accomplishments in my new business pursuits mirrored these feats. Not only did my bodily health empower me emotionally and physically, but my thoughts became clearer, and I tolerated stress much better. I realized everything was interconnected.

Our bodies are meant to be active. Sitting behind a desk for eight hours or more a day is not a natural state of physical health. While this cannot be avoided in many instances, the choices we make during the rest of our day can serve to maintain our physical health and prepare our bodies for success. Physical exercise has been shown to enhance neurochemicals believed to balance mood and reduce the effects of stress. Likewise exercise improves circulation to neural structures that expand interconnectivity between neurons and expand creative potential.[14] Unlike medications, which are an artificial path toward mood stability and creativity, physical exercise offers a natural and healthy approach. From this perspective the choice seems like an easy one.

Why do we find preparing our bodies for success so challenging? For one, the number of distractions we face on a daily basis can be overwhelming and deter us from our goals of becoming physically healthy. How many times do good intentions of exercising after work get squashed due to an unexpected appointment or obligation? In today's world so much happens throughout the day that hinders our commitment to be physically fit. For this reason my exercise routine occurs each and every morning before the rest of the world awakens. With sheer will and determination, I rise at three in the morning and lift weights in my garage before climbing four hundred flights of stairs on the StairMaster at my nearby gym. Then I resume heavier weight lifting to complete my training. This is my sacred time when the world is quiet. In the stillness of the early morning, I jumpstart my day in a manner that best aligns with my goals of success.

The second challenge related to preparing our bodies for success through exercise concerns the natural perception of the work involved. From personal experience I know that sticking to an exercise routine is difficult. But a funny thing happens after several weeks. After the initial struggle of changing our routine and overcoming soreness, our bodies respond favorably to the change by rewarding us with greater self-confidence. A few weeks later, our new routine becomes habitual just like any other activity good or bad, and ultimately preparing our bodies for success becomes incorporated into our lifestyle. At this stage proper physical care is no longer work or even habit but simply a manifestation of who we are. Properly caring for our bodies becomes a life priority no different from our other dreams and desires.

While proper physical exercise is a key component of preparing one's body, proper diet also deserves mention. Just as daily distractions hinder the adherence to an exercise schedule, social patterns of dining pose challenges to good dietary habits. The human body has a remarkable capacity to avoid starvation by storing unused calories for later use. Not knowing when the next meal may come, our bodies naturally play it safe by taking unused calories and converting them into fat. The problem lies not only in what we eat but also in the timing of our meals. In contrast to the traditional three meals a day with the largest one often being the last, the human body best performs when nutrition is provided in small portions every two to three hours. By changing eating patterns to this type of schedule, not only do we deter the body's tendency to store excess calories, but we also eat less as we become satiated sooner.

While the timing of our meals and their sizes clearly affect dietary health, the quality of our food is also important. A balanced approach to diet ensuring ideal amounts of proteins, carbohydrates, and fats provides the body with the right fuel to function at its optimal level. Fresh fruits and vegetables, along with vitamin and mineral supplements, further enhance physical function. I have personally adopted a dietary regimen based on a simplified and common-sense approach to healthy eating that my wife, as a personal trainer, has created for me. This practice, along with a commitment to daily exercise, has been life-changing to say the least. Having reached a state of optimum physical health, I could never imagine living any other way.

As we attain peak physical performance, we gain greater endurance to manage the demands of our day. We carry an increased capacity to handle problems and dilemmas without becoming stressed. Our mood remains more stabilized, and we can see a variety of circumstances from new and different perspectives. Our physical health is intimately connected to our mental and spiritual well-being, and our tendency to neglect our bodies can undermine our potential for attaining the success we desire. As a result we must prepare our bodies for success with the same degree of energy and effort we invest in mental preparation.

Preparation of the Spirit

Compared to the mind and body, our spirit represents a more intangible aspect of who we are. This section is not meant to instruct anyone on a particular spiritual viewpoint, and I certainly has no intention of influencing one's religious views and beliefs. Regardless of what one believes, intuitively we can appreciate that a life force and energy exist within us. This energy goes beyond what can be explained by the human mind and nervous system. This life source makes us wonder about our existence and purpose in life while instilling within us unique passions and desires and a sense of destiny. This is what we refer to as *spirit* or *soul*. And our spirit undoubtedly plays a significant role in fostering our creative mind and guiding us along the path toward success.

The inability to touch, see, hear, or otherwise tangibly experience our spirit invites numerous interpretations as to its influence on us. For many the spirit reflects the source of freewill and determines one's character. For some the spirit explains a capacity for one to exist beyond life as we currently know it. Indeed, if our spirit is energy, and energy and matter, can be neither created nor destroyed in total, science would likewise support the persistence of our spirit after death.[15] But no matter what philosophy or belief system one holds, no one actually knows for certain the total effect our spirit has on us and on others around us. As mentioned, spiritual energy likely plays a role in the law of attraction, bringing positive and negative energies our way as our spiritual energy vibrations beckon. Though research and evidence of such a phenomenon is increasing, these considerations will likely remain hypotheses for the foreseeable future.

From my perspective, I envision my spirit as pure energy. This energy permeates everything within me—my body, my mind, individual tissues and cells, and even individual molecules and atoms. Because of this diffuse presence, the spiritual energy I entertain affects everything else within me. For example positive energy allows cells within my body to overcome infection or illness more readily while negative energy may hinder this. Creative energies facilitate different neurons to connect with one another through similar creative frequencies. Thus, in considering how we might prepare our spirit for success, any activity that encourages positive thoughts and emotions and creative energy fosters success. And through these activities, our mind is further developed into a creative mind.

Because our spirits are energy, their influence is not contained within the constraints of our physical bodies. Each of our spirits emits vibrational energies that attract some energies toward us while pushing others away. This, in essence, is the law of attraction. But our spirit also has the capacity to connect to a higher source of energy from which all creative influence originates. Some may refer to this Creative Source as God while others may use terms such as Mother Nature, the Universal Source, or a variety of other terms. When we connect with this Creative Source with our own spirit, wonderful revelations can result. Problems without solutions suddenly have solutions. Innovative ideas appear, taking us in new and fascinating directions. The preparation of our spirit thus involves seeking an ability to foster positivity and creativity through belief and faith in our potential. By seeking guidance from the Creative Source, we naturally enhance these aspects within ourselves, and this readies us for an array of opportunities for success we might otherwise have ignored.

So how do we prepare our spirits for success? How do we foster positivity and creativity and connect with the Creative Source? Regardless of one's specific philosophy, spiritual empowerment routinely occurs through stillness. Quiet, peaceful periods of time free from interruption or distraction allow us to perceive our spiritual energies with greater awareness and focus. Reflection and relaxation permit noise to evaporate so the spirit's voice can be heard. And in this stillness, a connection between our spirit and the Creative Source becomes increasingly likely. These periods of time encourage us to look within rather than to interact with our environment. The preparation and strengthening of the spirit emanates from these internal practices as we ponder our own desires and hope to connect to the wisdom of the Creative Source.

A variety of practices exist that are used by individuals to empower their spiritual nature. Prayer is a common spiritual practice as is meditation. Guided imagery, progressive relaxation, and yoga are some other methods people choose to use in this regard. I use journaling as my exercise for spiritual empowerment and preparation. In fact I have two journals that help me strengthen my inner spirit, deepen my spiritual desire, and connect with a higher Creative Source. These are my gratitude journal as well as my dream journal. In my gratitude journal, I reflect on successes and revelations from the past for which I am grateful. While this activity strengthens my belief and faith, it also encourages humility and appreciation. In my dream journal, I invite my spirit to dream as big as it wishes. This activity encourages spiritual creativity and expansion, which in turn help me connect with the Creative Source. Through both of these journals, I not only infuse my spirit with creative energies but also direct my spirit toward character traits I value.

Inherently we have a drive and instinctual desire to grow and progress. In preparing our mind, we strive to enhance our knowledge and creative abilities in thought. In preparing our bodies, we seek to improve our endurance and strength while optimizing health. And in preparing our spirit, we pursue greater understanding of life's purpose while continually trying to become the best version of ourselves. Each of these areas contribute significantly to our ability to turn dreams and ideas into successful realities, and all are integral parts of the creative mind, strengthening our ability to conceive, believe, and achieve the success we desire.

Create a Powerful Day

In order to prepare one's mind, body, and spirit for success, planning and commitment are required. The manner in which one prepares speaks volumes about the eventual success that will be achieved. Personally I have found consistency enables me to best prepare all the areas of my life that are important for attaining my goals and dreams; however, everyone is unique. Some people may achieve better results through variety. Regardless, creating a schedule that fosters the creative mind thorough preparation is essential in achieving one's potential for success. This is what I refer to as a *powerful day*.

As you complete various chapters throughout this book, I encourage you to create your own powerful day, allowing time for various activities and tasks that foster success. You may in fact create a weekly or monthly schedule as well to ensure all activities are covered. In addition to listing various tasks to help you prepare your mind, body, and spirit, consult the sample of my typical powerful day that is provided below as a guide. Feel free to use my typical daily schedule as a template, or creatively orchestrate your own. The key is to be prepared for the success you desire. In the words of Ralph Waldo Emerson, "People only see what they are prepared to see."[16]

- **Exploring Passions**
  (five minutes daily)

  What are you passionate about? Interestingly I ask many people this question, and a dumbfounded look often appears on their faces. The problem for many is they have drifted so far away from a creative mind, they have become numb in perceiving their inner dreams and desires. To realize your potential destiny and attain the heights of success, you must find what will rekindle your inner passion. Many of the other activities in this book will assist you in this regard, but at the same time, it is important to reflect on the things that truly excite and motivate you.

  Passions are activities or subjects that completely consume your attention. Therefore, asking yourself which activities cause you to lose track of time is a great start in identifying your passions. Likewise, explore subjects in which you are highly knowledgeable since we often eagerly learn about topics in which we have a passionate interest. Finally, continually feed your mind new activities and information. Perhaps your passion has yet to be uncovered. By being consciously aware of things in life that trigger your excitement and interest, you will soon identify your true passions, and passions are always linked to success. These reveal our uniqueness and the path to our potential destiny.

- *Daily Study*
  (thirty minutes daily)
  Preparing your mind requires a continual input of information and knowledge. In order to grow and advance, our minds require new pieces of information and data that can be applied in a variety of creative ways to foster success. Whether we are starting a new endeavor or pursuing career advancement, constant learning is an essential ingredient for the creative mind. Setting aside some time every day to educate yourself ensures your mental abilities are not only progressing in knowledge but also actively engaged to consider creative opportunities.

  While detailed and thorough study should be pursued in the industry or field related to your desires, learning in other areas is also important. For example in my endeavors related to entertainment, I often apply concepts from business, marketing, social networking, and law to foster greater success. Developing a thirst for knowledge empowers the mind and prepares it well for ongoing achievement. As you grow your mind, you will likewise grow your potential for success.

- *Create a Daily Exercise Routine*
  (thirty minutes or more daily)
  Physical health plays a key role in a creative mind and in the pursuit of success. Not only is it difficult to focus on your dreams and desires when you feel poorly, but good health and physical fitness provide self-confidence, self-esteem, and the energy needed to persevere through challenges and obstacles. I believe exercise should be approached from the perspective of making a lifestyle change. In other words exercise

is not simply to attain a goal such as a specific weight or performance measure. Such goals are often helpful, but exercise should be in the daily routine of a successful lifestyle. The morning hours before the world is awake serve as the best time for me to ensure I exercise every day. Whatever part of the day works for you is fine. However, the time scheduled for exercise should be sacred. Don't allow other demands to infringe upon this time. Turn off your smartphone, iPad, laptop, or any other communication devices that might interrupt your workout. By dedicating daily time solely to exercise, you will soon find this time to be both stress-relieving and energizing. If monotonous routines bore you, mix up the types of exercise you do. The key is to commit to making physical activity a part of your day—every day.

- ***Eat for Success***
  (permanent lifestyle change)
  Everywhere you turn, recommendations for a variety of diets exist. From my perspective, keeping things simple allows me to eat healthy and prepare my body for success without becoming overly focused on what and when I eat. For example I ensure I get adequate proteins, carbohydrates, fiber, minerals, and vitamins while limiting fats, sugars, and preservatives. Fresh fruit and vegetables form a significant part of my diet as a result. In addition I eat small snacks or portions every two to three hours rather than eating two or three larger meals a day. These two practices keep me energized and healthy, allowing my body (and mind) to perform at its best.

In a society struggling to overcome an obesity epidemic, eating healthy foods in proper portions is rarely practiced. Many restaurants serve oversized amounts of food cooked in excess salt and oil in order to provide flavor. In reality portions should be the size of your palm or smaller. Select baked, grilled, or broiled options over fried selections when possible, and consider adopting a pattern of smaller, more-frequent meals. Drink water instead of sugary or highly caffeinated drinks. And keep alcohol (which also has a great deal of sugar) to a minimum. In making these changes, you will notice a marked increase in energy and stamina, which will result in enhanced abilities to achieve.

- *Making Time for Quiet Stillness*
  (fifteen minutes daily)
  My time for quiet stillness occurs in the early morning. I will reflect on the previous day, the week, and past successes. I also consider new possibilities, ideas, and dreams. During times of reflection and relaxation, I keep several journals that help me focus on a particular subject of reflection. For example as I write in my gratitude journal, I consider everything for which I am thankful. In my dream journal, I create a wish list of future desires. One fosters humility while the other promotes creativity and belief. Each, however, strengthens my spirit in different ways, and the peaceful reflection offers an opportunity to connect with the universal Creative Source.
  You do not necessarily need to journal to practice this exercise. I find converting my thoughts

and emotions into words helpful as it increases my attention and memory of the content and provides a resource for reflection later. However, many other types of quiet stillness and personal reflection are possible. Prayer, meditation, and other strategies are just as effective. Whatever practice speaks to your unique self and to your beliefs and perspectives should be adopted since this will have the most profound effect on preparing your spirit for the journey of success.

Bobbie Celler's Powerful Day

- 3:00 a.m.: Awaken, lift dumbbell weights, and perform abdominal exercises at home
- 4:00 a.m.: Manage e-mails/messages; journal; study vision board; create daily activity wish list
- 5:00 a.m.: Cardio exercise, weights, and steam shower at gym
- 6:30 a.m.: Command three ideas that will help move me closer to my goals
- 7:00 a.m.: Arrive at work; attend meetings, seminars, lectures, filming, client appointments, etc.
- 5:00 p.m.: Family time with wife and daughters
- 7:30 p.m.: Personal time for studying, sharing, and reflecting
- 9:00 p.m.: Bedtime

Create Your Own Powerful Day

_____

_____

_____

_____

_____

_____

_____

_____

_____

_____

_____

_____

_____

Chapter Five

Cultivating Willpower and Determination

In attending community and local art shows, I am continually impressed by the talent and skill of many visual artists. From photography to oil paints on canvas, the ability of these individuals to capture the essence of an image in their mind is inspiring. On occasion I have spoken to a few and discussed their aspirations, their dreams, and even obstacles they have encountered in their art careers. Interestingly most of the ones with whom I have spoken are incredibly passionate about their work. They harbor intense desires to express themselves through their art, and they enjoy a capacity not only to dream but to express their dreams in an elaborate fashion. But equally interesting is how many refuse to consider changing their approach to achieving success. Many of these artists carry the belief that eventually their works will be appreciated, and, regardless of advice they may receive from others, they are dedicated to pursuing the one path they believe will culminate in attaining their goals.

Based on this description, such artists indeed reflect a level of determination and commitment that is admirable. Let's face it—they are willing to put their personal expressions of art in front of others to be judged, critiqued, and analyzed. Without question this takes a bit of a thick skin. But the tendency to be uncompromising in their perceived path toward success misses a key component of the willpower and determination required to be successful. Success-related determination must be combined with the energies of a creative mind so adjustments may be made along the way. Being committed to a goal does not mean blindly pursuing a plan without any awareness of one's environment. The creative mind seeks alternatives in its determination to attain success. The journey never proceeds in straight line but instead zigzags through a complex course of events.

In this chapter we will discuss the importance of determination and willpower as well as how the creative mind utilizes determination in achieving goals. So far we have identified our passions and developed ideas and dreams that align with our unique destiny. We have recognized the power of positive thinking and the exploration of creativity as a means to attract success to our lives. And we have developed a strategy to prepare our mind, body, and spirit in order to pursue success to our best ability. In other words the destination has been identified, and we are set to travel. All we need now is to put fuel in the car. In considering the transformation of ideas and dreams into successful realities, creative determination and willpower represent the fuel we need.

The Importance of Adding Determination to Desire

Imagine purchasing tickets to see a once-in-a-lifetime concert. The event is being held in a city several miles away, so you arrange for hotel accommodations, block out your schedule for that weekend, and drive your car to the concert. But just before you arrive in the city, a major accident blocks the freeway, preventing access to the concert. Unfortunately the concert will begin in a couple of hours. What do you do? Knowing the opportunity to attend the concert will not likely present itself again, you ask yourself how much it means to you. Do you accept fate and sit in traffic? Or do you creatively stretch your mind and will your way to finding a solution? You might have the desire to attend the concert, but do you have the determination to make it a reality?

Determination originates from the Latin word *terminus*, which means "a limit or a boundary." Determination thus means we take away and eliminate any potential boundary or limit in order to achieve success. In other words nothing will stop us. We make what seems terminal and finite into the limitless and infinite. No single word or trait is more important in the pursuit of success. Determination is a core characteristic of the creative mind and reflects the outright refusal to give up on one's dreams and desires. When determination is combined with desire and passion, no roadblock can withstand its power.

Often we fail to have the willpower and perseverance in pursuing our dreams of success. We clearly see our destination, and we have planned the steps of the journey to take us there. But as obstacles and barriers begin to appear, we lose belief and faith. Negative thoughts begin to enter our minds and attract the very circumstances we wish to avoid. And slowly we allow our desires to weaken, settling for what fate has to offer us instead of exerting our own will. In such situations neither the destination nor the dream is flawed. These still reflect our unique passions and destiny. The only problem lies in the path we have chosen. Just as the freeway to the concert was shut down due to an accident, the path we chose to pursue for success may not be the one we should pursue. This is where determination and perseverance come into play.

Determination always finds a solution to any given problem. The answer may not be right in front of us or immediately apparent, but somewhere a different path leading us toward our goals exists. In regard to the concert, perhaps an alternative route off the freeway offers an opportunity. Or maybe another form of transportation such as a train may be available. The key is to combine your creative mind with the power of determination so that innovative and amazing solutions may be realized. Whether it's over, under, around the side, or from the back, determination will find a way to get us to our destination. And in the process, we gain greater belief and faith in our own abilities and in our ideas and dreams.

No matter how creative we may be in devising our own plan of action, the universe or Creative Source always knows the fastest way by which we can attain our goals and dreams. If we lack determination, we falsely accept our path as the only way to achieve success. Once we encounter an obstacle, we more readily relinquish our pursuits rather than considering alternatives. But with determination we not only consider other possibilities but are more likely to connect with the Creative Source. This occurs because determination encourages open-mindedness. Thus the ability to increase one's level of determination is another means by which we further develop a creative mind while turning desire into tangible results.

The Origins of Determination

In my life I have experienced how circumstances can affect one's determination from different perspectives. Early in my childhood, my parents divorced, and I went to live with my mother. Both my parents were originally from New York, and while my father soon remarried and moved away, I remained with my mother and sisters in the area. Interestingly my father came from a very wealthy background. His parents were multimillionaires, and all of my cousins on his side of the family enjoyed extremely nice lifestyles. While my cousins rode in fine cars and lived in stately mansions, my family lived in poverty, struggling to make ends meet between welfare supplements and part-time jobs. Short of a phone call from my father on my birthday, I received no attention or anything else from him. I even recognized his promises of gifts to be just as empty as the mailbox I would repeatedly search.

But this lack of support as a child awarded me many unrecognized benefits. I became responsible, autonomous, and independent as a result of this unlikely blessing. Having little to lose and everything to gain, I gained determination and perseverance. Despite being the black sheep of my father's side of the family, the resistance and disapproval I felt from my relatives fueled my desire to succeed. In addition to wanting to prove to myself I could overcome these obstacles, I wanted to show everyone else I could surpass all expectations. It was this degree of determination that propelled me through college and into law school. No obstacle could have deterred me from achieving these goals.

Things changed after I began law school, however. At age twenty-one I received access to a trust account from my paternal grandfather. He had arranged this financial support for all ten of his grandchildren. Over a ten-year period, I received approximately $300,000 divided into monthly installments. The money was enough to meet my needs easily through law school and served to provide additional comforts as I began working as an attorney. But interestingly something changed as access to the trust fund occurred. The money proved to be enough to squash my previous level of determination, and I became relatively content existing in my current situation. In essence the trust fund handicapped my willpower and drive to push forward. Because my needs were being met without significant effort on my part, my passion for greater success diminished along with my determination.

By the age of thirty, I had burned through all the trust-fund money and had failed miserably while trying to perform what I now refer to as *noncreative law*. The lack of desire and determination had transformed my initially creative mind into one lacking passion. The moral of my story is not meant to imply that money and a creative mind cannot coexist. In fact wealth often provides us the means by which we can enhance our creativity through practical opportunities. But my story does demonstrate how our experiences and situations can significantly affect our level of desire and determination. People are always strongest and most determined when they are backed into a corner. With little to lose and everything hinging on their own efforts to succeed, levels of determination increase. However, when comforts and provisions are given to us without any effort on our part, we risk losing our intensity of perseverance. The key is to maintain a creative mind regardless of our external influences. The creative mind remains hungry and determined regardless of the circumstances and fosters an attitude of perseverance, always pushing ahead toward growth and progress.

Once again I found myself with little money and resources except for my own inner desire to succeed. After reaching this low point in my life, I chose to bet everything on my own dreams and desires. With a few dollars to my name, some may have predicted I would never again reach a level of success, but deep down I knew I would. Determination and perseverance pushed me forward moment by moment, day after day. And each day I moved closer and closer to the goals I had established and toward my dreams of success. Through these experiences I developed a creative mind and chose to use positive thinking and determination to convert hopes into realities. I had the same dreams after completing law school, but the key difference between then and my present situation was my level of determination. I refused even to consider failure as an option.

One important dilemma concerns how to maintain high levels of hunger and determination even after great levels of success are attained. Many individuals achieve great success only to lose it after a period of time due to complacency. And then after losing it all, they once again attain success as the hunger returns. The thought that keeps me forever determined involves the residual $37 I had when things were at their worst. In my journals I reflect on this period and the sequence of events that occurred thereafter. This reflection reminds me how our level of determination can change depending on the urgency of our condition and the degree of faith we have in ourselves and our dreams. In regularly performing this exercise, I help ensure I remain hungry and committed to pursuing my goals further and further.

Determination, perseverance, and willpower come rather naturally for some individuals. They have an innate sense of pride and belief in themselves, which manifests itself as a dedication to their pursuits. Regardless of whether we have this naturally or not, each of us can increase our level of determination. If we have experienced periods of failure and success in our lives, reflecting on these situations can be incredibly helpful. They highlight the importance of perseverance in fueling our desires and transforming them into achievements. But if success has been elusive, other ways also exist to enhance determination. Our own genetic makeup and personal experiences are not the only influences on the strength of our willpower.

In addition to our own personal experiences with failure and success, stories and examples of others can also be sources of inspiration that increase our ability to persevere. After all our own experience forces us to believe we can overcome obstacles if we persist in our efforts when success occurs. Similarly, our belief in our abilities also grows as we see others accomplish similar tasks or overcome remarkable barriers to excel. A strong belief and faith in the ability to succeed empower determination, and this can be nurtured through our own experiences or through the experiences of others. Because of this fact, identifying inspirational figures and stories as a means to enhance one's willpower is an effective tool.

What or who inspires us to become more determined? Personally I have images of several individuals on my own vision board. These include people like President Obama, Warren Buffet, and others who have overcome adversity to excel to the top of their fields. Appreciating the struggles they suffered in their ascents, I feel inspired to overcome my own challenges. In addition, knowing others have conquered problems much larger than ones I will face empowers my faith in my own abilities. Every time I see their images, I gain motivation to persevere in my own daily challenges. If they did it, so can I.

Inspirations and motivations energize us to act and strengthen our determination to succeed in the process. Both achievements from our past and those of others can serve as a means to make us more determined individuals.

In addition to experiences and natural personality traits, determination also increases with practice. Just as our endurance improves the more we exercise, so does our willpower. For example when I encountered challenges earlier in my life, a greater sense of doubt developed within me. I wondered if the barrier was some sign indicating I was on the wrong path. Despite my doubts I persevered, and over time I came to realize these barriers were not warning signs but instead opportunities to grow. Now, when a challenge appears, my demeanor remains calm, and I look for the learning opportunities within the challenge. Through this my willpower and level of determination remain steadfast. In part, past experiences have strengthened my perseverance because I have stronger belief and faith. However, being determined to succeed has also become a natural part of my daily behavior. The more we practice determination, the more natural it becomes as part of our daily approach to problems.

The origins of determination are several and involve our natural ability to persevere, experiential influences based on past achievements, the influence of others on our beliefs and faith, and the frequency with which we exercise willpower. By understanding these origins, we can develop strategies to increase our dedication and commitment to achieving success. Determination fuels our passion to achieve our goals despite obstacles and challenges. And it remains an important ingredient in fostering greater belief and faith in our future success. With the aid of determination, the creative mind can turn our dreams into living, breathing realities.

Determination Versus Self-Control

By this point we have discussed determination from the perspective of perseverance. This viewpoint naturally implies an assertive posture pushing through barriers, overcoming challenges, and taking action to circumvent roadblocks. But determination has a twin brother that is more passive and restrained than assertive. In fact the term *willpower* is often used in the context of self-control when referring to abstaining from an undesirable behavior or suppressing an unwanted impulse. Though self-control may not offer the same fuel to turn dreams into successes, personal restraint does clear the path, enabling greater focus without distractions. As a result self-control fine tunes our determination with greater precision, making our efforts increasingly successful.

Self-control can be viewed as an alternative form of determination. Instead of being determined to achieve a goal, one is determined *not* to give into an impulse. In considering our plans and goals, impulsivity distracts us from our mission. Despite setting our sights on our desires of success, we become enamored with other images or activities along the way. As a result we never reach our destination. Self-control therefore represents an important aspect of determination, enabling us to remain attentive and to persevere toward the destination we originally desired. While determination erases boundaries preventing us from attaining our dreams, self-control reestablishes limits that allow greater clarity and efficiency in our pursuits.

During my college years, I was determined to complete the curriculum within three years instead of four. Through solid preparation I developed a plan allowing me to achieve this goal. As you might imagine, the number of distractions during those formidable years was significant. College parties, road trips to sports games, and other social events often lured me from my studies. But with the determination to achieve my educational goals, I not only asserted energy into a heavy course schedule but also exhibited self-restraint from participating in these appealing opportunities too frequently. The combination of self-control and determination allowed me to fulfill my mission and achieve my goal.

In today's world many cultures, including American culture, encourage impulsivity to a great degree. The ability to attain credit easily provides the means by which we can have what we want now instead of later. Plastic surgery offers immediate cosmetic changes rather than pursuing body sculpting through diet and exercise. And, in some instances, medications and pills provide seemingly quick fixes as opposed to more-natural and healthier long-term solutions. By giving in to these impulses, we fail to recognize the weakening of our self-control. And with weakened self-control, our tendency to stray off-path naturally increases.

Over the last several decades, diagnoses of attention deficit disorder (ADD) have skyrocketed. The reason for this is debatable among health professionals, but one leading theory involves a behavioral perspective. As technologies have encouraged progressively shorter snippets of our attention, our minds are increasingly less adept at maintaining long-term focus.[17] Handwritten letters evolved into e-mails and then into texts and tweets. YouTube videos are being increasingly viewed instead of full-length television programs and movies. And we now demand information almost instantaneously from a variety of Internet devices. All of these changes have served not only to reduce our attention span but to foster greater impulsivity as well.

Self-control empowers our determination and perseverance by strengthening our ability to focus on long-term goals without giving in to our urges. This does not imply that shortcuts or efficiencies in attaining our goals should not be pursued. Often the creative mind reveals new directions through which our dreams may be realized more quickly. But sacrificing long-term goals for short-term wants undermines our potential to fulfill our destiny. Impulses are best viewed as limits on our ability to succeed. If *determination* refers to the removal of limits, self-control serves to remove the limits of impulsivity from our lives. In this way self-control is intimately linked to our ability to persevere.

An important area where self-control is needed, particularly in today's fast-paced world, is patience. When success fails to come quickly despite our efforts, we have a tendency to become discouraged. When this occurs we lose desire, and our determination starts to weaken. The discouragement comes from a sense of failure in part, but this sentiment also emanates from a lack of patience for the creative mind to develop new opportunities and directions for success. When we are passionate about a dream, and we fuel this passion with strong determination, nothing can stop us. The dream may not be realized the next day, the next week, or even next year. but the positive energies and willpower of the creative mind will align circumstances that facilitate their transformation into actuality. By having a strong sense of self-control, we avoid the discouragement that comes with impatience and maintain a healthy dose of the determination needed to succeed.

Developing and Maintaining Strong Determination

Perhaps you are one of those individuals who naturally has a bulldog personality and pursues every goal tenaciously. Even if you are not, determination and perseverance can be strengthened through a variety of techniques. By tapping in to the origins of determination, your willpower and self-control can be bolstered to pave the way for success. Despite obstacles you will persist in your efforts supported by strong belief and faith in your ability to excel. Despite distractions you will remain focused on the prize through more-effective self-control. Instead of seeing limits, you will become limitless. Invest energy and effort into the following exercises, and you will progressively enjoy increasing levels of determination in your pursuits.

- *Reflect on Past Failures and Successes*
  (fifteen minutes weekly)
  This activity has provided me with incredible insights over the years. Past successes help empower me toward the achievement of future goals while highlighting the power of determination and willpower. Such successes further strengthen my confidence and deepen my faith and belief that my dreams will materialize. Both of these aspects of examining past successes make me more determined to move forward in my

pursuits. At the same time, reflections on past failures can also show how a lack of perseverance prevented me from attaining a goal or, more commonly, bring to light a more creative approach to pursue. Both aspects of this exercise encourage greater determination.

This reflective activity can be done as often as you like. I frequently review the same past failures and successes simply to remind myself of the importance of having strong willpower. For example I always remind myself of when I had only $37 on credit and how determination turned that moment of apparent failure into future success. Whichever failures or successes you find motivational will benefit your abilities to persevere. I would recommend performing this exercise at least once a week. After all determination adds fuel to the fire, and making sure your tank is full is important.

- *Identify and Study Inspirations*
  (ten minutes daily)
  People and events that inspire me change constantly. That is not to say past inspirations do not hold power in developing my determination to succeed. However, new inspirations provide freshness and variety that enhance my motivation to persevere. Most of the time, my inspirations involve individuals who have achieved major successes within areas of interest to me. In other instances a person who has overcome incredible odds to excel as a result of sheer determination creates a powerful sense of awe. I review and study these inspirations in a variety of ways. I will post images of some inspirations on my vision board so I

will see them frequently throughout the day. Other inspirations are in story form, and I pull them out once a week or so to remind myself of determination's power. In both instances I am striving to make these inspirations more tangible and real so they empower my own willpower and ability to persist.

In identifying your inspirations, be on the constant lookout for individuals, circumstances, and occurrences that speak to you. Look for that unique quality of willpower and determination in others so you may materialize this important concept within your mind. Once you have identified an inspiration, consider ways in which you can remind yourself of it often. Vision board images are excellent ways to use inspirations to build determination, as are videos and audiotapes. For example when driving a long distance in my car, I listen to inspirational stories of determination. Just as determination fuels our desires, we must find ways to fuel our determination. Inspirations are excellent ways to accomplish this.

- *Reward Your Own Perseverance*
  (periodically, at least monthly)
  There are two ways you can generally encourage good behaviors. One is to punish antagonistic behaviors through penalties, setbacks, and other negative consequences; however, this fosters negativity, which is less than ideal for developing a creative mind. Alternatively, positive rewards can be provided to encourage desirable behaviors. One exercise in building greater determination involves rewarding yourself when you persevere through a challenge or obstacle. When

moving past a barrier, you likely have such a sense of relief and a desire to move ahead that you neglect to take the time to acknowledge your level of determination. Reflecting on your willpower and giving yourself a reward for continuing toward the goal provides positive incentives for future perseverance.

Humility is a beneficial trait as it promotes graciousness and thankfulness. But at the same time you should foster determination by recognizing your efforts and rewarding them accordingly. At least monthly, reflect on obstacles you encountered in achieving recent goals. Examine the level of perseverance you exhibited, and then reward yourself for your efforts. The reward does not need to be anything dramatic, but it should be something you thoroughly enjoy. Perhaps a small accessory item you wanted or an extra hour of sleep on the weekend. Regardless of the incentive, make sure the bar for rewarding your determination is set high enough. The incentive for future determination is directly proportional to the level of past accomplishments. While this exercise may be subtle, it has great potential for developing positive behaviors of perseverance.

- *Practice Patience and Self-Control*
  (ten minutes weekly)
  Disciplining ourselves to be patient and to control our impulses is always challenging, especially when surrounded by others who often give in to their urges and whims. However, in order to develop focused determination toward your dreams and goals, you must practice self-restraint and identify potential areas of

weakness. Much of the ability to develop patience and self-control comes from the ability to establish goals and to pursue them efficiently without distractions. For example if you plan to invest in a new marketing strategy, this goal may be delayed if money is spent on other items rather than saved for this purpose. Goals provide opportunities to practice patience and self-control because they require your complete attention to be realized in an expedient fashion.

Success occurs over a period of time. Rarely does it happen overnight. As you establish daily and weekly goals, list potential pitfalls that may sabotage their achievement. Once these pitfalls are identified, list behaviors that are counterproductive to attaining your goals. The more often and completely these potential setbacks are identified, the less likely you will be to give in to distracting impulses. In addition, establish long-term as well as short-term goals and review them often. Patience is strengthened as you continually focus on long-term goals and remain on course toward their achievement. And if you go off course, you can quickly realize your faults and get back on track.

While this exercise can be performed daily as you reassess your goals, at a minimum you should assess the accuracy of your direction weekly. Every time you self-correct and get back on track, you strengthen your determination through more-effective self-control.

- ***Always Push for That One Percent Shift***
  (*five minutes every morning*)
  The essence of life is growth. Within every living

entity, the desire to push forward, advance, and evolve through positive change exists. Thus the desire to attain success, wealth, goals, and dreams is natural and completely synchronous with life itself. Determination simply encourages this continual growth, no different from a lone flower that struggles to push through a crack in the sidewalk. By understanding this we can foster determination by purposefully striving to advance every day no matter how small the gain. Each day you should commit to making progress toward your goals through some type of defined effort.

I like to think of this activity as the "one percent shift." By making progress toward my goals by at least one percent every day, eventually I will reach a tipping point where suddenly the goal or dream becomes realized. One drop a day in a bucket eventually causes it to overflow; the same concept can be applied to our pursuit of success. By continually striving to be your best, you will eventually realize your goals. Therefore, when you create your schedule for the day, identify specific, objective tasks that can help you make progress toward your dreams. This continuous one percent shift forward from where you are currently demands determination. Though hares may seem to be passing you in your pursuits, the determination of the tortoise ultimately succeeds. Commit every morning to achieving a one percent shift in your life toward your dreams.

Willpower and determination are naturally perceived as inherent qualities in some individuals—we either have it or we don't. But this perspective is limited and fails to acknowledge our ability to foster determination through our efforts. Indeed some people seem to enjoy a natural fire within themselves to persevere, fueled by self-confidence and a will of iron. But determination can be enjoyed by everyone as a means to turn dreams into successes.

Through examining our own past successes, we can gain confidence in and commitment to our future efforts. By seeking inspirations we can convince ourselves we too can reach new heights through perseverance and determination through the examples of others. And with self-restraint and patience, we can develop a character dedicated to success that is absolutely unstoppable. Add these activities to your daily and weekly tasks, and in time you will enjoy increased levels of determination and greater willpower in overcoming anything standing in your way.

Chapter Six

Create Your Roadmap to Success: The Importance of Planning

A few months ago, I found myself driving around Central Florida in a rental car. I routinely travel to Orlando for business, and in fact many of the video productions I attend require I travel into the area once a week. This afternoon was unusual because I had time to spare before my next meeting, and since it was a beautiful day I decided to take the scenic route from the airport to the studio rather than going my usual route. Rather than checking a map, I let my instincts guide me toward my destination. I pride myself on having good directional skills and knew my intuition would get me close to where I was going even without the GPS. Plus a little adventure is always good for the soul. Besides, I had an hour before the meeting. How far off course could I travel?

Forty-five minutes later, I found myself in Kissimmee, well south of the recording studio. What I had failed to appreciate was the number of lakes throughout Central Florida and the inability of any road to travel in a clear north, south, east, or west direction for any length of time. After incorrectly estimating my path of travel for miles through the curves and twists in the road, I eventually swallowed my pride and checked my GPS. I arrived at the studio on time...but just barely. What had started out as a peaceful and pleasant drive on a sunny day had quickly turned into a stressful, pressured rush through freeway traffic on Interstate 4. And this all resulted from the lack of a map and a plan.

Success requires a number of ingredients including desire, passion, preparation, and determination, and it requires a degree of planning. Every detail of our journey need not be defined, but having a sense of direction, specific goals, and a plan of how to achieve these goals provides us with guidance. Planning is thus important in making our ascent efficient and productive, and planning holds us accountable by always providing a measurement by which we can assess our progress.

Though plans are not fixed in stone, they do provide a framework for us to consider when pursuing our dreams. Without them we are sure to take many wrong turns, waste precious amounts of time, and possibly never reach our dream destinations. As with any journey of endurance fraught with distractions and struggles, we must develop a plan to achieve the success we truly desire.

Planning a Career of Success—The Basics

Some have defined success as pursuing an endeavor hat fulfills the soul from within. In other words true success emanates from our internal dreams and desires, and its pursuits are naturally pleasing to us. In contrast we are guaranteed to be miserable if we pursue something that is poorly aligned with our likes and pleasures. Unfortunately we have all met many people who fit this latter description. Perhaps at one point of their lives, they dreamed of pursuing their real passions and becoming successful, but somewhere along the way, they relinquished that dream and settled for something less enjoyable. When we consider success, we must identify activities and interests that generate deep satisfaction from inside and pursue them wholeheartedly. Only then will we be able to best align our pursuits with our own unique destiny. With this in mind, the first step in planning our success involves self-reflection and self-evaluation to determine the type of success we want to achieve. Different people thrive in different situations. For example some individuals excel when operating within a structured environment with a limited set of responsibilities. Their ability to focus on a task without distractions enables them to reach new heights of creativity they otherwise could not have attained. Others prefer a more expansive landscape where their creativity can explore limitless boundaries in developing ideas never before considered. Both scenarios have exciting opportunities for success, but identifying which one best serves us is important before we develop our own roadmaps. The basics of success planning demands we have a solid understanding of the type of success we desire.

The first question thus involves whether we prefer an entrepreneurial path or an employee's path as part of our journey. These paths are not necessarily mutually exclusive. In some instances individuals may gain experience and knowledge as employees before pursuing their own interests alone. Being an employee within an industry may serve to reduce personal risk initially while acquiring various assets. Such assets may not involve only financial considerations but also intellectual and relational ones as well. Once these individuals are better prepared, they then pursue an entrepreneurial direction. Despite this mixed approach involving roles as an employee and entrepreneur, their need for individual autonomy and expansive creativity ultimately best characterizes them as entrepreneurs.

In addition to determining which roles allow us to best reach our desired destinations of success, an examination of our level of risk aversion is also important. Individuals who are aversive to risk tend to be more conservative, to prefer the security of a steady wage and benefits, and to feel more comfortable in a structured setting where responsibilities are defined. Others who are less risk-aversive are willing to take chances in order to hit it big. The freedoms of owning one's business and charting its course have both pros and cons. Advantages include greater autonomy and potential profitability while being able to create without limits. But the presence of increased risk means the potential for significant losses and setbacks as well. Ultimately risk aversion reflects an inherent personality trait, and neither approach is right or wrong. The correct approach is simply the one that best aligns with your unique personality and desires. If you choose your path accordingly, you will be much more likely to attain the success you crave.

The second basic consideration in success planning involves determining the general direction we wish to travel and the goals we wish to achieve. Defining passions, talents, and levels of risk tolerance is important. Looking within ourselves to find these traits helps align our roadmap with our hopes for success. But similarly important is looking outside of ourselves and examining the landscape around us. The creative mind rarely locks us in to a single path or a solitary pursuit. Life, as well as success, is about change, adaptability, and growth. Taking our inner characteristics and dreams and blindly pursuing them neglects consideration for the ever-changing environments around us. Planning for success thus requires a comprehensive perspective that examines not only inner desires but the outer landscape as well.

In decades past the norm for many people was to graduate high school, attend college, decide on a major course of study, and then look for a job upon graduation. If students use the same strategy today, they are essentially rolling the dice to determine their chances of success. In recent times many people have graduated with academic degrees having limited job markets. From a positive perspective, they may have followed their interests and passions, but they failed to match these to current job environments. Following our interests without any regard to market demand is like grilling sirloin for a party of vegetarians— no matter how well the steak is cooked, no one is eating dinner.

The best way to approach success planning after identifying our inner desires and strengths is to study the landscape. I like to think of this as starting at the finish. If we realize success is attainable for everyone, then focusing on the end-product certainly makes sense. Which industries are thriving or are expected to thrive in the future? If one's passion is sales, which items will be in demand? For decades the health care and insurance sectors have demonstrated great opportunities for jobs and success. Similarly, information technology and related advances in technological hardware and software have been steady growth areas of opportunity. Whether one has an entrepreneurial or employee perspective, examining the environment is crucial to aligning one's passion with opportunity. And this formula greatly enhances the chances of success as we plan our strategies.

Business and Career Planning

With an understanding of our passions, our talents, and the landscape of opportunity, we have defined a clear direction for success planning. If we have an entrepreneurial spirit, then planning will proceed with a focus on potential business opportunities. If we prefer advancing our career as an employee, then we will seek positions that align with our ultimate career goals. In both instances the art of planning requires a few specific considerations. First we must have an entrance strategy into our field of interest.

Second we must embrace our creative potential and apply it to the industry we have chosen. And last we must initially consider competitive pressures so we know where new and innovative explorations may lurk and fill that niche in the market. Practical steps of planning are required, but developing additional success strategies that allow our creative mind to participate in the planning process increases our likelihood of true success.

Let's first consider entrance strategies as part of our success planning. As an individual wanting to succeed as an employee in an existing organization, gaining a solid footing in the company is important. How do we differentiate ourselves from the masses? Amazingly many people fail to pay attention to the requirements an employer outlines in the application for a position. This oversight of details instantly tells an employer a great deal about a potential candidate. When I seek new employees, I require three things: a résumé, a cover letter, and a typing test. The latter tells me a person's level of literacy, his or her propensity to make mistakes, and his or her efficiency. But I dismiss more than 90 percent of the applications because the potential employee failed to submit one of the three items for consideration. What incentive do I have to hire a person who demonstrates from the beginning that they cannot attend to details?

At minimum a good entrance strategy requires focusing on the specific needs of the position. Employers like individuals who are detail-oriented and follow instructions well. Similarly they are impressed by individuals who persevere and go above and beyond what is required. As part of an entrance strategy, we should seek to separate ourselves from other candidates for the position by anticipating the requirements of the job and showing our talents in those areas. On one occasion I interviewed an individual for an administrative position hat required expertise in mail-merging abilities. When she arrived for the interview, not only had she brought all the required documentation, but she also presented me with a binder that contained a large collection of various mail-merge samples she had created. She immediately had my attention and interest.

As an attorney representing hospitals for a variety of insurance claims, occasionally I am invited to attend certain hospital functions. Several months ago I attended a social event where the attendees affiliated with the hospital gave a brief introduction of themselves. Amid the more-standard introductions, a young man took the podium and stated his name for the crowd. He then proceeded to explain succinctly his skills, education, and experience as well as his desire to attain a position of employment in health care. Not only did he have a captive audience, but he also demonstrated creativity, innovation, and motivation. Now that's an effective entrance strategy.

Entrepreneurs must seek effective entrance strategies when considering a new business and market. Like employees, entrepreneurs must differentiate themselves from other businesses in the industry, and a creative strategy can provide significant benefit in this regard. Because success is available to everyone, and because creativity is a limitless commodity, examining the competition is not something I routinely incorporate as part of my business planning. But for entrepreneurs entering a field, examining the competition initially serves an important task. By knowing the current state of the market, I can more readily recognize new opportunities for creativity and innovation. After this initial assessment of the competition occurs, however, I generally never look back at my competitors again. After all I am not competing for success among a pool of other individuals. I am challenging myself to best utilize my creative mind in exploring new and wonderful concepts that include the creation of a useful and profitable product or service.

In business and career planning, both entrepreneurs and employees utilize the creative mind to make what currently exists better. The creative mind is always looking to enhance value, make improvements, and expand opportunities. If we follow our passions in industries that are in high demand, the opportunity for success is astounding regardless of the competition. By using creativity we find ways to differentiate ourselves as unique. Room for improvement is always possible regardless of how great an existing concept may be. Creativity is the secret weapon bridging the gap between our desires and effective business and career planning. And effective planning combined with determination is guaranteed to enable us to reach our goals.

Even in seemingly saturated markets, new opportunities exist. In 2008 a cyclist struggled to negotiate his bicycle through the ice and snow along Boston's streets while traveling to a rental car location. As he journeyed he noticed multiple cars parked alongside the road not being used. Two years later the cyclist, Shelby Clark, founded a company based in San Francisco named Relay-Rides, which allows customers to rent cars from local owners, and the owners receive a significant percentage of the rental fees. Since the inception of RelayRides, other car-sharing businesses have opened as well, but Clark, through creative genius, realized a new opportunity within a market that was thought to be fully mature.[18] The creative mind always opens new doors where many believe the barriers are tightly shut. Effective entrance strategies thus benefit greatly from the power of the creative mind.

In addition to an entrance strategy and creative considerations, practical steps to success planning are certainly necessary. For both entrepreneurs and employees, developing the necessary infrastructure is essential. For example individuals seeking positions with an organization need to have the necessary skills and education for the position. They need well-polished résumés, solid references, and detailed cover letters. Likewise proper attire is necessary to make a good impression, and examples of one's work go a long way in demonstrating abilities that may not be apparent in an interview. Detailed preparation continues to be an essential ingredient in turning a plan into eventual success. And even after the initial job is obtained, continued preparation and creativity are needed for one to excel further toward their goals.

For entrepreneurs many other practical steps are required in business planning. While the potential for success is much greater as the sole owner of a business, the responsibilities are more numerous. But contrary to common beliefs, success planning for new companies can be easily achieved without the use of tremendous resources. Incorporating a business, locating an office, securing necessary telecommunications, and establishing a business pro forma can be completed inexpensively with guidance from the Internet and other sources of information. In fact these aspects of setting up a business are so easily acquired many choose never to formally create a business plan. However, this accounts for many failures among entrepreneurs. No matter how many basic foundations are put into place, nothing replaces a solid business plan when pursuing success.

Business planning provides us with a clear roadmap and destination for our entrepreneurial journey, but in addition it gives us an opportunity to explore ideas, contemplate alternatives, consider potential barriers, and, of course, be creative. In the process of defining a business concept, a market, the competition, and many other variables, our creative mind naturally begin, to expand our thoughts and consider new possibilities. Like an employee who recognizes some shortcomings when preparing his or her résumé and portfolio, entrepreneurs often recognize new challenges when devising business plans. Identifying these dilemmas early allows us to consider alternatives strategically at a time when other pressures and stresses are absent. In this situation as well, detailed preparation facilitates success by enabling the creative mind to anticipate problems and provide insightful solutions.

Whether we wish to start a new business or attain a position with an existing company, thorough planning remains an essential step in our journey to success. The more prepared we are, the more likely it is that we will foresee challenges and develop effective resolutions. Planning engages the creative mind and awards it the chance to participate in our efforts. Dedicating time and energy to success planning is therefore an essential ingredient in fostering our future successes.

The Importance of Branding and Marketing

Within the scope of business and career planning is a subcomponent of success planning related to marketing. What exactly is marketing? Many people confuse it with advertising, which is essentially a means of presenting one's services, one's products, or even oneself to a potential audience. This reflects a one-way channel of information where one entity provides details and another passively receives it. Marketing, on the other hand, reflects a more active process. Not only are the details of a product or service described, but marketing engages a potential audience and tells them why this particular product or service is what they need. Likewise marketing actively seeks to know the exact needs and wants of its clients. Advertising is important, but in order to attain success, we must actively engage our audience. Marketing is the means by which we accomplish this.

Consider two bakeries that sell cupcakes to consumers. Cupcakes are trendy. Having done their homework and identified their passions, both companies have chosen a business for which great demand exists and that naturally engages their interests. One company chooses to purchase television time for advertising, distribute flyers at local community events, and wait for word of mouth to enhance their sales. Indeed some growth is experienced, but the realization of success-related goals is slow. The other company, however, chooses to solicit feedback from their customers via e-mail, makes a dozen phone calls daily to evaluate consumer responses, and holds contests for new cupcake ideas. In the process the second bakery realizes a large demand for gluten-free cupcakes and reduced-calorie cupcakes within their market. As a result new lines of cupcakes are developed, and growth accelerates dramatically. The first company chose to advertise; the second chose to market.

Marketing infuses energy and action into your business plan, thus driving change and progress toward success goals. Many individuals fail to recognize that success demands such an active perspective. When we exhibit positive thoughts and energy through action, the law of attraction becomes much more powerful. Through action we pull events toward us that eliminate obstacles and facilitate future success. In contrast the same positive thoughts combined with passivity may attract positive events into our lives, but the speed with which they occur is significantly reduced. Passivity lacks the energy of action, which accelerates the process of dream transformation into realized success.

In order to know which actions to take, we must know our markets. For entrepreneurs these markets reflect customers. If we only advertise to these individuals, we tell only our side of the story. But if we reach out and engage these customers in some type of dialogue, we not only express the information we want them to know but at the same time we learn about their needs and wants. In turn we gain knowledge of how to proceed to best serve their needs, facilitating success in the process. Our creative mind can then use this information to develop new ideas, which beneficially differentiates our business from others. Creative innovations hold the key to accelerating our success, but marketing provides the input that guides our creativity in the most productive way.

For individuals choosing to pursue employment as a means to achieve their dreams, the same concepts of marketing apply. While customers represent the key audience for entrepreneurs, employers represent the market for those focused on career planning. Creating a résumé and attaining credentials and even letters of recommendation are important activities to convey one's qualities. But, like advertising, these efforts are primarily passive. Marketing implies a more-active role in not only expressing one's own skills and talents but similarly finding out what employers want. Based on the number of individuals who submit employment applications to me without typing tests, I can verify the majority of people seeking jobs choose advertising over marketing.

Just as entrepreneurs need to differentiate their businesses from others in the industry, so must individuals seeking career positions with organizations differentiate themselves. But career differentiation without a clear guide as to what employers want is like collecting baseball cards without knowing their values. Research employers before sending in résumés and additional materials. Identify which qualities, skills, and characteristics seem to align best with the company's vision and goals. While nearly every organization sees value in individuals who are detail-oriented and dedicated, nuances within specific companies can provide additional clues about the type of employee desired. By learning as much as you can about a company before applying for a position, you increase your ability to tailor your abilities as well as your information, which can significantly increase your chances of landing the job. That's the power of marketing.

In discussing the above aspects of marketing, branding is crucial to success. Appreciating that an entrepreneur's company and goods reflect a specific brand shows common understanding. But at the same time, we should realize we too are a brand when we apply for a position within an organization. Just as Coca-Cola has come to represent an iconic brand of soft drink, we should also strive to develop a brand consistency of the values and skills we wish to portray. Remember, you are your own brand!

In researching the talents and traits employers want, we can refine our personal brand to meet expectations. In the process we create a differentiated brand unique to ourselves yet well-aligned with the demands of our market—our employer. Branding demands a well-defined vision, consistency, and a determined effort to create an image as developed through one's marketing plan. Regardless of whether you are an entrepreneur or an employee, brand development should be an essential process in which you engage your creative mind to meet your goals.

In developing our roadmap to success, business planning provides opportunities for practical considerations and creativity. Logically identifying steps that must be taken to achieve our dreams is important; likewise the opportunity to infuse creative energies into this planning process facilitates innovations, provides a means to overcome obstacles, and enhances our passions while attracting positive energies and events our way. But in addition a marketing plan and the development of our unique brand accelerate our journey to attaining success. By appreciating our inner desires and talents as well as the market's needs and demands, we learn to adapt and improve in efficient directions. As a result goals are realized more quickly, and our dreams of success materialize before our eyes. By choosing to engage our markets actively regardless of who they may be, we allow success to come our way sooner rather than later.

Practical Steps to Effective Planning

In order to utilize the following exercises of planning your success effectively, you must first take an inventory of your abilities, your skills, your dreams, and your aspirations. Are you an individual who thrives best under structure, or do you prefer an open canvas upon which to create? Does your vision of success involve progressing through an organization, or does it involve starting a company from scratch? What is your ability to tolerate risk and to deal with the unknown? As you reflect on the person you are and your passions, you will identify a path that best suits you. For some individuals taking a journey as an employee for a while may eventually culminate in an entrepreneurial pursuit. Or, in other instances, success is not defined by company or career success but by having tremendous flexibility and freedoms in schedules for other pursuits. Only you know which path best reflects who you are and the successes you desire.

Once you have identified your dreams and goals and the approach that is best for you, the following exercises can help you develop your roadmap to success and keep you on that path. Success follows an unpredictable course, and the process of success planning will be an ongoing endeavor. Obstacles will appear, environments will change, and perhaps you may further refine your dreams as knowledge and experience come your way. Regardless, success planning will consistently provide you with the steps needed so you may invest energy and action in a productive direction. Knowing your destination is great but having the map to get there is even better.

- *Define and Refine Your Brand*
  (fifteen minutes a week)
  In order to create effective success planning, you must define your brand. Whether this is your business, a product, your services, or you as an employee, differentiating yourself through branding provides the means to catapult yourself into the success your desire. In deciding upon your brand, apply creative strategies to identify how to make yourself or your market better. What innovative ideas can be applied to existing ones? What voids exist in the market? Branding in part reflects your unique traits and abilities, but it also involves researching the market and determining how these skills can be best utilized in reaching your goals. Therefore branding is an essential first step in the planning process.

  When you first start planning, study the market and yourself, and define your brand. Then allow this vision to saturate all aspects of your business plan. Initially this process will take several hours of research, information gathering, and reflection. But once it's established, a half hour a week or so can help you continually refine your brand according to the needs of your market. Refining your brand is a key part of success planning as environments are constantly changing. In order to reach for your goals continually, your brand must evolve over time. Stay current with your field of interest and market, investing time weekly into new trends and changes. When you maintain a vibrant and living brand, the steps of your business plan can remained focused on a realistic target of success.

- **Create a Formal Business/Career Plan**
  (annual commitment)
  Once your brand is established, you need to create a formal business plan. While services exist to aid you with this activity, I strongly encourage you to attempt your own version before enlisting the services of a business-plan or résumé writer. The process of developing your own business or career plan allows you to consider new obstacles and possibilities you would not have considered otherwise. For entrepreneurs, business planning forces you to study the market, research competitors, examine financial options, and explore many other important aspects. For employees, formal career planning demands you evaluate your own talents and skills, assess potential employers, and devise ways to improve your marketability. Though the development of formal business and career planning takes many hours, the reward for such an investment is immeasurable. Without a thoughtful and detailed plan, the ability to attain success becomes increasingly more difficult.

  I also strongly recommend reassessing your business or career plan on an annual basis. Similar to branding, the environment of your market changes, which often requires revisions in ongoing success planning. Likewise, personal and professional growth naturally occurs, changing your perspectives, skills, and dreams. Daily and weekly adjustments in your plans occur through actively pursuing success, but I suggest a more formal approach to planning revisions once a year. Taking dedicated time to reevaluate your plans and goals offers a chance for self-reflection, study, and creative considerations in greater depth. Often this practice can provide significant results in redirecting your efforts toward attaining greater success.

- *Three Daily Ideas for Progress*
  (ten minutes every morning)
  As part of my daily routine each morning, I challenge myself to develop three new ideas that will advance me toward my goals that day. This exercise provides a couple of advantages. First I automatically engage my creative mind in exploring new possibilities for attaining greater success. If an obstacle has presented itself, then this exercise forces me to consider new ways around it. Or, if progress has become stagnant, this activity demands I invent different approaches. Success is directly dependent on how effectively we use our creativity; and I have found insisting upon three new daily ideas for growth is beneficial.

  Second, and more relevant to business and career planning, this exercise forces action. Having a plan for success is great, but without action the plan is unlikely to be very effective. Demanding three new ideas each day requires prior ideas to have failed. And how can an idea fail if we have never put it into action? Success demands action. The purpose of success planning assumes action. If I have failed to infuse energy and action into my plan, I will immediately realize it when I consider developing new approaches. In essence formulated these ideas each day holds me accountable for at least attempting past ideas.

- ***Deadline Accountability***
  (ten minutes weekly)
  In keeping with the theme of accountability, effective plans should have specific deadlines for each step. Deadlines should be realistic, but they also should be measures of self-assessment. After all what benefit does success planning provide if we fail to assign a timetable to our accomplishments? Stating you will become vice president of an organization might be a great goal, but unless a deadline is associated with this achievement, a sense of urgency may not exist. You might aspire to own a million-dollar corporation, but this dream may remain elusive unless you insist on attaining the goal within a certain period of time.

  Plans for success change over time. More-efficient paths may become evident. New opportunities may arise. Deadlines are a way by which you can reassess your plans to ensure they remain the best and most efficient means to attain goals. When a deadline comes and a goal is not attained, reflection and reassessment are needed. Perhaps you have failed to be as active as you should be. Maybe creative adjustments are needed to devise new strategies or targets. Success planning requires monitoring and evaluation over time, and having deadlines forces you to perform these activities on a regular basis. I suggest examining deadlines weekly in order to maintain a focus on your progress. By performing this exercise weekly, your ability to stray too off course is minimized.

Regardless of whether you aspire to succeed as an entrepreneur or as an officer of a corporation, success planning remains an important and essential tool to accomplish goals. Many individuals enjoy great passions and desires for success, and many have shown powerful creativity and determination. But when these qualities lack a good sense of direction, energy and efforts can be wasted. The ability to allocate time, energy, and other resources efficiently and effectively toward our dreams becomes impaired. Spending time to create a solid brand and plan represents a wise investment and could mean the difference between realizing success and simply hoping it will appear. Create a plan, infuse it with action and energy, and continually reassess progress accordingly. In doing so the ability to stay on course will be greatly enhanced, as will be the opportunity to reach the desired destination.

Chapter Seven

Working the Plan

Fast, focused, faithful, and flexible. These four words symbolize the key components needed to put our plan for success into action and achieve our dreams. The term *fast* refers to our ability to use our time and other resources efficiently so that goals are attained expeditiously. Being *focused* highlights our ability to stay on task without succumbing to a variety of inherent distractions that seem to be ever present. *Faithfulness* describes our ability to be committed to our plan while pursuing it with a sense of urgency. And *flexibility* reflects our ability to adapt and change aspects of our plan continuously as conditions dictate. A success plan is both essential and beneficial in helping us progress in our journey to the top, but a plan without action is like a sailboat without wind. Great potential must be accompanied by great effort in order to realize success.

In this chapter we will explore these core components of working a success plan. Starting with dreams and desires, we have described the power of the creative mind in promoting positive thinking, the law of attraction, and visions of success. We have considered creating tangible images of our destinations as well as thorough preparation and planning. And we have identified determination and willpower as driving forces to push us toward our destination. With these pieces in place, one key ingredient is needed to well-equip us with the tools needed to reach our potential. By understanding how best to work our plan through measures of efficiency, commitment, and adaptability, the final piece of our success puzzle can be put into place.

Fast—Seeking the Most Efficient Path

Of the many valuable assets we possess, time is by far our most precious resource and commodity. Unlike many assets, once spent, time is impossible to retrieve. Though we might be able to adjust future schedules and other activities to have additional time later, the fact remains that once used, time is gone forever.

Using time efficiently should be an important goal for all of us in our ascent toward success. Efficiency allows us to arrive at our goals quickly, which facilitates subsequent steps of our plan to be pursued. As a result our plan becomes increasingly energized with action because we are eliminating wasteful efforts worth little value.

For many people living in large cities, a daily work commute in their car is part of their routine. Imagine a person waking up and preparing for work feeling energized to tackle any obstacle. As they get behind the wheel and pull out of their driveway, their mind is full of creative ideas about progressive actions they will take. As they negotiate the streets of their neighborhood, the increasing momentum of the car mirrors the momentum of new ideas for success. But suddenly they merge onto the interstate and struggle with stop-and-go traffic for the next half hour before finally arriving at work. While they may regain their initial momentum temporarily, the time wasted on their commute serves to diffuse the energy of their passions. Inefficiency and wasted time drained them of their initial vigor.

Pockets of wasted time are quite similar to stop-and-go traffic. We lurch forward only to suddenly apply the brakes again. Instead of smoothly traveling closer to our destination in a progressive fashion, we erratically make fragmented progress in spurts. Rather than being empowered and motivated by our progress, we instead become frustrated and irritated. Now imagine if the same person chose to leave their house two hours earlier, exercise at a gym in the city close to work, and spend the time normally spent in traffic planning their day's schedule. Instead of being frustrated, they would be energized and prepared. Instead of lacking motivation and momentum, they would hit the ground running as soon as they arrived at the office. What made the difference? Efficiency.

As a definition I describe efficiency as the fastest means to attain a goal. If we are somewhat efficient in our approach to our success plan, we will likely attain a slight degree of success. If we are efficient most of the time, we will likely attain moderate degrees of success. But if we strive to be 100 percent efficient, our chances of success and the scope of our success will increase exponentially. Efficiency and success do not enjoy a perfectly linear relationship because success breeds success. The more efficient we are with our time, the greater the number of successful opportunities we experience. And each successful opportunity may open several other doors for additional opportunities. For this reason, as we move from being somewhat efficient to being completely efficient, our ability to realize success grows by leaps and bounds well beyond what we might have predicted.

I learned to appreciate the relationship between efficiency and success early in my professional career. When I first began, my days consisted of a routine between 9:00 a.m. and 5:00 p.m. of seeing clients and creating legal documents. But as I started assertively working my plan for success, I noticed some ways in which I could still meet my routine duties while investing greater energy into achieving other goals. Each of these efforts would then lead to additional opportunities for my law practice to grow, and the success I was realizing seemed to be progressing steadily. As I increasingly began to devise better uses of my time in pursuing my success plan, a flood of opportunities suddenly appeared.

Today my business schedule consists of a variety of meetings with patent attorneys, entertainment promoters, software developers, production directors, health-care administrators, entertainment promoters, musicians, and celebrities. While previously my workday was limited to a narrow list of activities, it now encompasses a broad scope of interests. How did my life change so drastically in just a few years? I became more efficient in working my plans for success. As I made time for each step of my plan, new opportunities would appear, and this opportunity would expand into several other ones. A little bit of efficiency is good in terms of success, but being maximally efficient is incredibly powerful. As a result we should strive to continually achieve better use of our time each day in working our plans for success.

Focused—Avoiding the Distractions

Being focused on our plans for success naturally relates to our ability to use time efficiently. When our attention is consumed by our specific tasks and goals, we complete them faster, thus enhancing the momentum and energy of our efforts. Unfortunately many thieves exist that attempt to rob us of our ability to focus. Phone calls, e-mails, and unexpected arrivals request our attention throughout the day. An array of responsibilities demands our focus, ranging from family relationships to work duties to personal time. While efficiency seeks to schedule the time spent in each of these roles as well as possible, being focused allows us to get the most out of the time allotted. One is quantity, and the other is quality. Thus when we are attending to one specific action, we are completely consumed in that task, allowing us to complete it not only quickly but accurately as well. Both results enhance our ability to work our plans for success effectively.

The key to being focused is to avoid distractions, and this can be accomplished through assessing common interruptions and making changes in our behaviors. For a long time, I wanted to become more physically fit. I would make promises to myself, affirming I would attend the gym every afternoon after work. But inevitably, unexpected interruptions and distractions would interfere. An appointment would run past its allotted time. Traffic would hinder my ability to get to the gym and keep other commitments. Every week my ability to focus on my promise was limited because distractions got in the way.

A simple change made all the difference in the world. I changed my sleeping hours and committed to waking early to begin my day with an exercise session. Before the rest of the world was awake, I focused solely on my physical health without any interruptions whatsoever. Within a few weeks, I enjoyed increased energy, which allowed me to focus better on many other activities throughout my day. I soon realized that by handling several other tasks during these quiet hours of the morning, I could enhance my attention in many other areas as well. Not only could I address an increasing number of goals in my plans of success, but my focus allowed me to infuse greater creativity into potential solutions and opportunities. Indeed this scheduling change increased my efficiency, but it also awarded me the chance to focus completely on activities I had previously neglected.

I now call this period in my mornings my "three hours of

power." During this time I plan my day and establish specific goals I wish to accomplish. I create my schedule of events and appointments, review important decisions, and still attend to my physical health. These peaceful moments of uninterrupted time have made significant differences in my abilities to focus on details and achieve many goals. In addition, by dedicating this time immediately after awakening, my mind and body are refreshed. This further enhances my creative abilities as well as my level of attention. Since adopting this behavior, the number of dreams and desires that have materialized have increased exponentially. Because I am both more efficient and focused in working my plan, success has become reality.

While the early morning hours work well for me, different schedules may prove to be more attractive for others. The goal of being focused in every daily activity to the greatest extent requires an analysis of distractions throughout the day. Many distractions are so subtle they may go unnoticed. A few weeks prior, I had a meeting with a legal client at my office. Though we met for only an hour, my client must have checked his phone for messages no less than twenty times. If asked, he likely would have believed he was attentive throughout the entire meeting. But the number of pauses in his comments and delays in his responses due to glances at his smartphone suggested otherwise. My guess is he had no awareness of the tiny interruptions this caused.

E-mails previously represented similar distractions for me. Throughout the day I would check them, and the time taken to read and reply detracted from my ability to have consolidated periods of time. As a result my productivity was less than it should have been. Once I recognized this habit as distracting, I devised a change. Now I read and reply to e-mails in the morning and during a couple of dedicated time periods before noon. E-mails received after midday are reviewed only if they are marked "urgent." This schedule has worked well, allowing an appropriate amount of attention to be given to e-mail correspondence and enhancing my ability to be more productive the rest of the time. Without these self-created interruptions, my focus increased along with my daily progress.

Because each of us is unique and different, a set schedule to enhance our focus does not exist. Refining our ability to focus and stay on task requires us to take an inventory of our daily activities routinely and examine where potential distractions and interruptions may be eliminated. Often we can make relatively minor changes in our schedule or in the sequence of events throughout our day to improve our focus and attention. And as a result, we become more efficient, more productive, and increasingly successful. The time spent on our success plan improves qualitatively because our dedicated attention is enhanced. Without the distractions our creative mind becomes even more powerful, tapping in to the universal Creative Source more readily. As a result our advancement toward success becomes accelerated in a very short time.

Faithfulness—Maintaining Drive and Urgency

We have explored determination and willpower as being key ingredients in the climb toward success. Determination provides the energy that bridges the gap between desire and realization. And faith empowers determination as well as positive thinking in our abilities to achieve our goals. In considering faithfulness in relation to working our plan for success, faith relates to a powerful belief in our plan to move us closer to realizing our dreams. This faith is manifested in our drive and our sense of urgency to move closer to this dream every day. Therefore, identifying our drive can allow insights into how faithfulness can be increased and how we can keep a sense of urgency and hunger about attaining our goals.

In identifying our inner drive toward success, we must recognize it can change over time. What drives us now may later change, reflecting our maturity and progress along our journey. Believe it or not, my initial drive to become successful began at the age of three. At the time I was seated in a burgundy-leather office chair as my mother spoke with her divorce attorney. My father had chosen to pursue a relationship with another woman, and we were left with essentially nothing. As I sat in the attorney's office, comprehending the conversation was of course impossible given my age. But even so I was able to recognize something was wrong, and I also recognized the power the law held in determining our fate. My dream to become an attorney started with that moment in time as a result of my desire to have control over my own situation.

Because of such childhood experiences, my initial drive toward success was linked to a need to control my own future. I became faithful to my dream of becoming self-sufficient and autonomous. My drive and my faithfulness thus became intertwined, and I was able to attain the goals I established. But in time, as I gained greater confidence in myself, my drive for further success changed. As I became a father, my drive to achieve became attached to a desire to show my children anything was possible. My faithfulness in being a good parent and teaching my children how to pursue success became a more potent driver of my dedications. Time and time again, I have found that when we recognize what drives and motivates us, we can easily identify where our faithfulness lies. And faithfulness is what keeps us on course and hungry to reach our goals.

My drive for success today is completely different from my

initial drive as a child sitting in a law office. Instead of being driven by needs of self-assurance and control, I now pursue success purely for the love of creating something new and amazing. Being able to imagine the impossible and then creating the means by which it can become reality drives me more deeply and completely than any of my past desires. As I have matured as an individual, my inner drive for success has evolved. Instead of being dedicated to attaining greater control or to serving as a better role model, my faithfulness now lies in the aspiration to fulfill my own unique destiny through the power of the creative mind. The joy and sheer fun of creating and seeing creations emanate success motivate me to a greater extent now than any other past drives.

By being in touch with my own motivations, I readily know where my faithfulness lies. I am faithful to becoming increasingly successful for the love of creativity itself. The ability to develop innovative ideas is both the journey and the reward, and this allows me to maintain a sense of urgency in working my plan every day. When we recognize what motivates us, we can appreciate where our faithfulness lies. Perhaps we want greater social recognition or financial comfort. If so, we should be faithful in attaining fame or wealth respectively, and our plans of success should reflect this. Maybe several motivations exist, and our dedication spans a variety of goals. As long as we can continue to be efficient and focused, we can remain faithful to all of these. The important point is to know what drives us and to attach this motivation to our goals so faithfulness in action is empowered. If the task and the outcome are congruent with our desires, faithfulness and a sense of urgency are sure to follow.

One additional word regarding a sense of urgency should be mentioned. In discussing the development of our business and marketing plans, a major ingredient separating the successful from the unsuccessful involves the presence of action. Action and effort are required to energize our plans so success can be realized. But action is much like pushing a wheelbarrow up a hill. If the wheelbarrow is moving, momentum allows progress with increasingly less effort. Friction and minor obstacles have little power to impede our advancement. But if the wheelbarrow is continually stopping and starting, these normally insignificant forces have greater antagonistic effects on the climb. Not only is action necessary on our parts, but ongoing energy must be supplied to gain a strong momentum toward our goals.

Having a sense of urgency helps provide a continuous supply of energy and action in working our plan. Drive and determination help provide this feeling of resolve, but additionally we must perceive that a window of opportunity is closing unless we act quickly. Just as we strive to be efficient and utilize time most effectively by being focused, having a sense of urgency demonstrates our respect for time and the doors of success it can open. Similarly, urgency creates the momentum we need to help us overcome obstacles such as self-doubt, second guessing, and outside criticisms. When we are faithful in pursuing our mission and do so with resolve and urgency, we give little to no weight to these potential barriers to success. Having strong faith in ourselves and our plan enhances our actions, and our actions in turn reestablish our faithfulness.

Flexibility—Being Adaptable to Success

When we developed our roadmaps to success, our plans provided us with a guide of action and a series of steps that, if pursued, would likely lead us to a life of success. In the process of infusing this plan with energy and action, drive and dedication, we progress closer and closer to realizing our hopes and dreams. It remains important, however, to realize our roadmap is simply a guide. As we travel along in our journey, we may run into unexpected situations, obstacles, and barriers. New opportunities may also appear, requiring us to reconsider which path is most efficient. If we are too rigid in our adherence to our success plan, we may miss a chance to realize success more rapidly. Sometimes rigidity may even cause us to lose the opportunity altogether.

Flexibility is thus another important characteristic in working our success plan effectively. After all the universe and the Creative Source know the best path for us to attain the success we desire. If we are reluctant to consider alternative ways of reaching our goals, we shut off the creative mind, which is always open to other possibilities and considerations. While flexibility represents a core trait of creativity, rigidity is just the opposite. The more resistant we are to adaptation and change in how we perceive our course of action, the more closed-minded we become. In the process we suppress the very creativity we need to foster success in our lives.

Fortunately the more active we become in pursuing our plan, the more flexible and adaptable we become. Initially we begin to pursue individual steps of our plan as if checking off a list of grocery items as we shop for a dinner party. This mechanical and essentially noncreative beginning soon gives way to creative opportunities. We arrive home to learn one of our guests has a specific food allergy. So we must alter our plan and consider an alternative menu for dinner based on the foods we have bought. If we choose to remain steadfast to our original plan, at best we will have an unhappy guest, and at worst the evening will end with an ambulance taking someone to the hospital. But if we embrace the creative opportunity and alter our plan, the opportunity for success is quite likely. Being flexible thus invites creativity while allowing us to see new paths to follow.

In considering the ability to adapt and change in relation to circumstances, I find an analogy of an onion somewhat helpful. Many individuals create a plan for success and stare at it as if looking at the outside of an onion. The plan is a discrete entity that in total represents the path to success. The onion is uniform in color, solid, and round. Regardless of what is happening around the onion, it will continue to look the same from every angle, offering little flexibility or alteration in its appearance. Similarly, regardless of what transpires as these individuals pursue the steps of their plan, the plan remains the same—unchanging and rigid.

Others not only see their plan from the outside but are continually dissecting it and examining every intricate detail. Instead of being on the outside of the onion, they see every layer. If one layer fails to meet expectations, it can be peeled back, allowing other layers to appear. If one layer is bruised or discolored and fails to provide the taste of success, plenty of other layers exist, enabling the journey to continue. These layers symbolize the flexibility needed for true success to be realized as quickly and as completely as possible. While our plan is created as a single entity, numerous chances to adapt to changing environments exist. We must envision our plan not as a single, uniform object but as a multilayered, adaptable work in progress.

In addition to providing a source of creative exploration and expression, flexibility also allows us to enjoy variety in our lives. Though structure and routine can be reassuring and promote efficiency in many situations, a lack of variety often stymies creativity and hinders growth. If we fail to challenge ourselves with change, we tend to become stagnant, ignoring new opportunities for advancement and success. In contrast, as we embrace greater flexibility, change provides a different variety of activities and experiences that challenge our routines. Our schedules change, and we develop new skills and perspectives. New opinions are introduced, causing us to reconsider our views of the world and of our desires for success. Even reading this book offers the chance to explore new ideas and ways of examining your journey from a different perspective.

In comparing my daily schedule when I first opened my own law firm to my schedule today, the increase in day-to-day variety over a routine is readily apparent. Flexibility and adaptability are such key ingredients in my efforts to pursue success that arranging my schedule a week in advance is nearly impossible. Each day I develop a schedule in which half my responsibilities change constantly. Similarly, variety and flexibility are apparent on my vision board. Images are change weekly as additional dreams and desires are posted. As a result flexibility keeps my efforts toward success energized. The novelties that constantly permeate my activities, thoughts, and visions chase away any potential staleness of routine. And as a result, I pursue my plan for success with greater vigor and vitality.

Our plans for success are important, and their ability to motivate us, guide us, and lead us toward success cannot be stressed enough. However, even when such plans are intricately developed with great attention to detail, our ability to foresee every obstacle, challenge, and change is limited. Therefore flexibility must be practiced so we may adapt and change accordingly. By being flexible we invite even greater creativity and variety into our lives, which in turn fosters greater potential for success. The ability to adapt thus further invigorates us in our efforts to better pursue our plans for success.

Practical Exercises to Help Work Your Plan

The following exercises strengthen your abilities to be fast, focused, faithful, and flexible in your efforts to pursue your plan of success actively. These four crucial elements provide the energy and creativity needed to reach your goals effectively regardless of what obstacles and changes may occur. Though a plan is an effective guide for you to follow in your ascent, you must infuse it with action, energy, and creativity in order for it to be of benefit to you. The following activities help ensure you maintain a high level of these ingredients and apply them to your plan so success remains within your grasp.

- *Daily Efficiency Inventories*
  (ten minutes daily)
  In order to see, you must open your eyes. In an effort to become faster and more efficient in your pursuit of success, some assessment of your schedule and processes must be incorporated into your regular activities. Many people unfortunately fall into a rut while mechanically going through the same daily routines expecting to make miraculous progress. But without actively examining whether tasks could be performed more efficiently, we miss opportunities to enhance our success plans and optimally utilize time as a resource. For this reason daily inventories to seek better efficiencies should be undertaken.

  I perform this exercise each morning as I examine my daily schedule. Are the times allotted for various appointments appropriate, and does the amount of time align well with my priorities? Can any activities be consolidated? Can any serial activities be compartmentalized into a single block of time? Do better ways exist to accomplish my daily tasks? Is it more efficient for my long-range goals to have daily assistance? In time you will devise your own list of questions that will help you create a more efficient means to attain success. The important part of this exercise is simply to ensure you take an inventory of your actions regularly. Efficiency will improve only through careful examination and creative considerations.

- *Three Hours of Power*
  (three hours daily)
  As I have described, my three hours of power session occurs each morning before the rest of the world starts its day. The goal is to find three hours of focused time during which I can be completely attentive to a variety of tasks. During this time I focus on my physical health through exercise, and I manage several tasks related to my workday such as handling e-mails, preparing my schedule, and creatively examining my goals. Depending on my current priorities, I assign focused periods of time to a number of tasks that increase the quality of energy and effort awarded them. Likewise I attempt to eliminate potential distractions during this time that may later affect my attention throughout my day.
  While consolidating these three hours together is not required, I have found the momentum enjoyed from having this time consecutively enables me to be more productive. You may find you are most productive if you assign one hour at three different times

throughout your day. Whatever works best for your ability to focus and be attentive is fine. For example you may choose to answer e-mails all at once for an hour at the end of the day instead of attending to them in a more fragmented fashion. Or you may exercise in the morning for an hour and assign focused time to other tasks in the evening. Use your creative mind to best devise your three hours of power. Regardless of the schedule and practices you create, dedicating your focused attention three hours a day will result in dramatic improvements in your life. In a short period of time, your ability to work your plan and achieve success will accelerate tremendously.

- *Define Your Drive*
  (ten minutes monthly)
  Your ability to be faithful in your pursuit of success requires aligning your actions with what matters most to you. If you are not clear on your motivations and what drives you toward success, establishing faithfulness in action and a sense of urgency will be challenging. On the other hand, if you invest a small amount of time to reflect on your inner drive for attaining success, your motives will become clear, and you will strengthen your faith in your efforts.

  As I have mentioned, my drive to be successful evolved over time. I suspect your motivations will also. Therefore, periodically take time to reflect on the purpose of your pursuits. Why do you want to be successful? What does success mean to you? If you become successful, what will you have gained not only in status or wealth but mentally, emotionally, and spiritually? Does your current plan for success match these motivations well? Do the steps involved in attaining success reflect the values behind your motivations? The deeper you dig into these issues, the more aware you will become of your motivations for attaining success. Once known, your faithfulness (and energy) in your pursuits can be enhanced by ensuring your plan is congruent with your underlying drives.

- *Create Contingencies*
  (ten minutes daily)
  This exercise in flexibility and adaptability is important in a couple of ways. First, creating alternative plans in case roadblocks or obstacles appear facilitates greater efficiency since you are already prepared for the setback. Second, considering contingencies in your plans engages your creative mind to consider other possibilities for achieving a better path to your desired destination. The one thing that is certain in life is change, and the ability to predict change will always be challenging at best. Therefore, creating alternative options in your efforts toward your goals embraces flexibility and places you a step ahead.

I perform this exercise during my morning routine as I command myself to consider new ideas and possibilities for how to approach my success goals. Though part of my creative exercises, this activity also serves to maintain flexibility and increase confidence. As you look over your schedule for the day or week, ask yourself if some other way exists to accomplish the same goals of these activities should something happen. Try to anticipate unexpected outcomes and have an alternative plan already in place. This may be as simple as bringing your laptop to a lunch meeting in case a client gets detained in traffic or as complex as firing and hiring new staff for a specific endeavor. In creating contingencies we should allow our creative mind to explore broad options of change. This best promotes our ability to be flexible, and in the process we become more adept in pursuing success as we experience unpredictable environments.

Chapter Eight

Failures, Setbacks, and Obstacles: Success Opportunities

Ideas are said to be a dime a dozen. Simply perusing the Internet or talking with friends can help us readily identify a new restaurant concept, a new consumer service, or some innovative gadget. In many cases these ideas have real merit and potential benefit, but the majority of these concepts never materialize. Before a plan of action is even considered, potential barriers and obstacles surface and extinguish the passions for success before they have any chance to grow. Because we cannot see the path clearly, we relinquish our dreams, assuming we will fail in the process. Though we might say it is better to have tried and failed than not to have tried at all, in actuality we believe our efforts to avoid failure have high value. Because of this even imagined obstacles prevent us from taking action.

Why do most people never attain the success they deserve? Do they lack passion, desire, creativity, and commitment? In some cases these ingredients of success may be lacking or insufficient, but these deficiencies are not the most-common sources of failure. Often our own vision (or lack thereof) of exactly how success will be attained causes us to pause. We develop too many qualifiers, requirements, and safeguards before we take action, and as a result many of us never take the first step. Instead we remain paralyzed somewhere in between our dreams and our fears, and we forego the opportunity to attain the success we desire, choosing to play it safe. Unfortunately playing it safe shuts down the creative mind and usually closes the door to any potential success.

Obstacles, whether real or imagined, should not be something we fear. Instead barriers and setbacks should stimulate our minds to consider new possibilities, options, and opportunities. Roadblocks offer ideal chances to explore creative solutions and expand our skills and talents in overcoming current limitations. By changing the way we view obstacles, we invite positive attitudes that infuse us with energy to find other creative paths and strategies. By developing new alternatives of action, we gain greater confidence and faith in our abilities to attain success. And when we repeatedly overcome barriers in our lives, we foster greater determination and commitment to the success we desire. Despite the common perception of obstacles as hindrances to success, they are actually tools by which we enhance our abilities to achieve our goals and our dreams. A subtle shift in the way we perceive barriers to success can make all the difference in the world.

Changing Our Perspective of the Path

For centuries science and religion have clashed over certain issues. Common topics of debate involve the origin of earth and mankind, the existence of life after death, and the effects of spiritual powers over world events. The difference of opinions between these two fields of study does not simply reside in some fundamental set of beliefs about the existence of God or spiritual influence. Instead the difference resides in the measure of objective fact needed to validate belief. In other words science demands verified proof through the use of the scientific method, which focuses on objective facts. In contrast most religions are grounded in faith and a belief in a subjective perception. Interestingly this same difference between objectivity and subjectivity exemplifies the various ways people view obstacles when considering success.

People naturally want to see the end of the road. If we set out on a journey, we want to be sure the path takes us to our desired destination, otherwise our energy and efforts could be a total waste of time. Preventing inefficiency becomes such an important goal, we do our best to predict obstacles in advance and reasons why the path may not work. All of this occurs in an effort to save ourselves from poorly investing our energies in something that is unproductive. In other words we need proof the path will lead us to the success we want before we set out on our journey.

Without question, efficiency and productivity are important. Developing our success plan with the best use of our time and energy in mind guides us in the right direction. But efficiency and productivity are not the only guiding principles. We must also have belief and faith in our abilities to attain success. We must be dedicated and determined to persevere along the path, driven by our faith and beliefs. If we ignore these aspects of success and wait for proof that our plans will work, we will not only be waiting a long time but may also sacrifice many opportunities to realize our dreams in the process. Regardless of how badly we wish to see the path to success in its entirety, the world simply does not work this way. While we must utilize facts to devise the best plan we can, we must also passionately embrace our faith and our beliefs in our success and move forward.

If we have done our due diligence in developing a plan of success that is aligned with our passions and the external landscape, we can be reassured that doors will open for us as we actively work our plan. The actual path may not be the same as the one we expected, and undoubtedly obstacles and dilemmas will occur, forcing us to rethink our efforts. Our perspective of the journey will naturally change as this occurs. But instead of demanding proof, each step will bring us closer to our goals, and our faith in our future success will gradually expand, giving us greater confidence and reassurance. No longer will we be hesitant to proceed because we fear wasting our time. Instead we will persevere, believing success will eventually come even when setbacks and obstacles occur.

Our belief in our abilities to achieve success is in part objective and in part subjective. We may believe in our potential based on past experiences and successes (proof), and we may support the notion that everyone has the potential to achieve success through the use of the creative mind (faith). However, another subjective perception can prevent us from pursuing success and lower our sense of self-confidence. This subjective perception is fear, which I often describe as an acronym standing for "false evidence appearing real." Fear is likewise based on our past experiences as well as imagined uncertainty regarding the future. When present it can place the brakes on our progress and halt our actions. Whereas confidence and positive thinking expand creativity, fear constricts our ability to consider new possibilities and alternatives. It is thus important to foster not only a perspective supportive of success but one that readily identifies one's fears.

Fears essentially come in three main varieties. The first and most common is the fear of failure. Let's face it: no one likes to fail. When we strive for something and come up short, we naturally feel a sense of disappointment. We envision what others must think of us as a result of our failure. The more power we give these potentially negative thoughts, the more closed we become to exploring alternative options, and the less apt we are to persevere.

When we examine a challenge and anticipate failure, we must push forward and identify opportunities for success. Personally I twist any fear of failure into a potentially positive experience. If I fail, I know I will be forced to explore new options. In turn this will enhance my creative mind and ultimately make me stronger. Failure should not be something we fear but a chance to learn something new.

The second type of fear prohibiting success is the fear of poverty. For individuals who experienced prior personal struggles and lean times, fear can persist within their subconscious minds, reminding them of an unsuccessful background. Low confidence, poor self-esteem, and a lack of dedication can result from such feelings. Instead of this fear of poverty driving us toward success, these secondary emotions become self-fulfilling prophecies leading us further away from our dreams. This type of fear can even plague some individuals after they have attained a significant degree of success. Despite having proven they are capable of achieving their goals, somewhere deep within their psyches they still lack faith in themselves. Their fear of poverty serves as a magnet slowing pulling them backward, and every time an obstacle occurs negative thoughts resurface, causing a limited perspective of their abilities once again. If the fear of poverty exists, we must be sure to identify the extent to which we use it as a motivator for positive efforts and any negative effects it has on our self-perception.

Third, the fear of success, may seem a bit unusual. How can anyone fear success? Interestingly it is quite common and involves a fear of the unknown and concern about change. Success naturally brings change, and while much of it is incredibly positive, change itself can serve as a source of fear. What if the friends I have now no longer associate with me once I am successful? How will my friends and family treat me after I attain a greater status?

Will I be able to manage the increase in responsibilities? These and many other concerns regarding success can cause worry and anxiety when we have negative perspectives about change.

Change, however, should be embraced as an exciting and bold opportunity for growth filled with new opportunities to be creative. While mild anxiety can help us be more prepared for changes associated with success, excessive worry can lead to fear and paralysis, prohibiting us from progressing and growing. Adopting a healthy perspective envisioning change as beneficial to our goals is thus important.

How we perceive the journey toward our success greatly influences the way we view obstacles and barriers along the way. Objectively planning the steps needed to reach our goals is important, but we need not see the entire path before we begin. Faith and belief are necessary ingredients, and these are strengthened when we see our journey as a positive, exciting opportunity. Likewise each obstacle should be seen as a means by which advancement and maturity can be gained. Every barrier allows us to use our creative mind and become stronger in our degree of determination. By identifying our fears while placing them in a more positive light, we can overcome potential emotions that can deter our efforts. A slight change in perspective is all we need to get us back on track.

The Real Purpose of Obstacles

One of my most recent pursuits along my own personal success journey involved a conversation with an entertainment promotions expert. Through persistent determination I finally spoke with the promoter and explained my dreams related to a new entertainment tour. But instead of hearing my pitch as a possibility and an opportunity, he began to highlight my lack of experience in the promotions industry, my limited knowledge of running a national tour, and several other presumed shortcomings. In other words all he could see was a series of obstacles that immediately closed the door on creative possibilities.

After allowing him to express his negative perspectives, I asked him what experience he had with hologram entertainment, intermission musical concerts for business conferences, and social media interactives, which were all part of my entertainment concept. A notable pause occurred on the other end of the phone line. He had been so busy identifying my obstacles, he had failed to consider his own.

Obstacles can be used for a variety of purposes. In the case of the promoter, he had chosen to use them as a means to protect his own turf and to elevate his own talents. By showing me the obstacles he had overcome in his life, he perhaps subconsciously hoped to dissuade me from pursuing my dreams further. Obstacles, as I have mentioned previously, can be used to substantiate our own fears. In these instances barriers are used to falsely protect us from failure or other concerns. Obstacles can also be viewed as reasons not to move forward because fate is against us. In this situation setbacks invite negative thoughts, which in turn attract other negative circumstances in our lives. Fortunately none of these uses of obstacles represents their real purpose in our pursuit of success.

Obstacles serve two essential constructive purposes in realizing our dreams and desires. First, barriers and setbacks serve to enhance our skills and abilities in creativity, determination, and commitment. How can a person know they are committed unless challenged by difficult situations? How can we improve our abilities to solve problems creatively unless we have actual dilemmas to resolve? First and foremost obstacles offer chances to use our

creative mind and develop increasingly advanced skills in positive thinking, determination, innovation, and planning. Setbacks
should never serve as excuses to quit but instead be viewed as
educational tools that foster greater abilities to achieve success. If
the front door is locked, we can then explore ways to enter from
the side, around the back, through the chimney, or by digging
a tunnel. Barriers never suggest we take no for an answer but
instead demand that we exercise our creative muscles as a means
to find different paths to attaining success.

The second purpose of obstacles serves to highlight the presence of a greater Creative Source. When I reach a barrier that is
difficult to resolve, I immediately see a red flag. In some cases the
barrier has presented itself because I need to grow and advance
personally before moving forward. Perhaps I need new skills
and knowledge, or maybe the climate is simply not ideal for my
immediate goals. In other instances the barrier halts my progress
because another more effective strategy or plan exists to help me
toward my goals. After all the Creative Source always knows the
most efficient path in realizing our dreams.

A sudden obstacle that seems to indicate impassability may be
encouraging us to change our plans and pursue a different direction toward our goals. When this occurs I tend to stop and reflect
on alternative possibilities while remaining patient. In time the
direction will become clear as long as I remain positive and determined to continue my journey.

Obstacles therefore should not be viewed as hindrances, as
validations of our fears, or as a means to inhibit others. Obstacles
are simply present to help guide and protect us as we pursue our
ultimate dreams and destiny. Barriers help us develop additional
talents and foster the use of the creative mind, which progressively
allows us to overcome increasingly challenging hurdles. Likewise
barriers often direct us to travel a path that is more efficient and
more productive in achieving our goals. Despite developing our

own plan for success, deviation from the plan is often required since we may be unable to foresee future challenges and circumstances. When setbacks occur they often indicate that a slight redirection is needed so we may continue on our mission. I have known many individuals who have attained remarkable degrees of success, and each and every one has suffered many obstacles in their ascent to the top. Anyone who has achieved and maintained continued success has received their share of bumps and bruises along the way. My struggles came when I found myself nearly penniless, unemployed, and emotionally alone. I could have perceived these obstacles as reasons to quit but instead saw them as opportunities to change my life in a positive manner. As the old Chinese proverb states, the strongest steel is forged in the hottest fire. If we wish to attain great success, we must realize that obstacles are inevitable and the means by which we gain the skills, talents, and direction to make success a reality.

Wisdom in Handling Obstacles

As we meet challenges and obstacles, we will naturally gain important insights that can be used for later successes. I have certainly learned many important pearls of wisdom concerning the path of success through the many setbacks I have experienced. While everyone's journey is different, and each of us has our own unique set of setbacks from which to learn, sharing what I have learned concerning common challenges may be of some help. Some lessons learned are universal, and by way of example, hopefully I can provide some insights into how to best manage various types of resistance that are commonly faced. Barriers and setbacks will continue to occur, but by having some advance knowledge, our ability surpass these challenges will be enhanced.

One piece of wisdom I can provide involves the three phases

of resistance that are commonly experienced as we attempt to overcome barriers. From entertainment promoters to health-insurance executives, the same staged response occurs whenever I propose a solution or path that is contrary to the norm. Many challenges we face often exhibit similar patterns of resistance. When we recognize this natural pattern, obstacles become better understood and less intimidating. Knowing this also helps us develop greater determination and willpower since we appreciate that such resistance can be conquered. In time we become more accustomed to dealing with these challenges.

The first phase of resistance involves a complete refusal to accept any change. For example when I first present an alternative reimbursement concept from my clients to health-insurance representatives, their immediate response is typically, "We do not agree with you." It's difficult to negotiate when the other side simply refuses to consider a different point of view. For many people such a barrier would be a cause to forego any further effort, assuming the obstacle is impossible to overcome. However, with determination, this quickly gives way to the second phase where a slight shift in their perspective occurs. In the same example, after my continued explanation and solicitation, the insurance representative might eventually respond, "I see your point, but I still disagree." In essence the barrier has weakened, and I now have my foot in the door. Continued determination will usually force the door all the way open the majority of the time with creativity, positive thinking, and perseverance.

In the third phase, resistance dissipates as a complete shift in perspective occurs. After having time to consider the change, benefits and potential are seen. Resistance slowly yields to opportunity. In some cases this shift occurs due to a mutual incentive for change while in other situations repercussions resulting from a failure to change may encourage the shift. Regardless, determination remains the key ingredient facilitating this evolution from resistance to acceptance. Time and time again, I have seen dozens of seemingly impassable barriers gradually melt away. People need time to adjust to change, and presenting solutions to setbacks often demands major shifts in viewpoints. Recognizing the stages of resistance can help provide support for the continued determination and patience needed to overcome many obstacles.

Another notable insight regarding obstacles involves friends and family members. Concerning our dreams of success, we naturally want to share such desires with those we love and trust. Likewise we routinely need to lean on others when we experience challenges and difficulties. Because of this we assume friends and family are a great source of strength and empowerment when obstacles occur, but in reality family and friends can also unknowingly provide barriers to our success. Unlike people who have a less in-depth knowledge of our past history and background, friends and family know us all too well. Because of this they often make assumptions about our abilities to achieve success and overcome barriers. Unfortunately these perceptions are often inaccurate and tainted by a false lens through which family and friends view the situation.

Different factors may cause family and friends to make false assumptions about our chances of success. In some instances people close to us embrace a competitive spirit when it comes to our achievements. When this occurs our advancement or success can be viewed subconsciously with envy or resentment. Rather than viewing our opportunities with optimism, pessimistic opinions may be offered. If these opinions are our primary source of support and encouragement, we may become dejected and disillusioned by weighing them too heavily. Therefore, sharing our dreams and desires for our future with friends and family members must be done with some degree of caution.

Interestingly, generational dynamics can play a role within families fostering a perpetual negative perspective concerning success. Consider a father who once pursued his dreams but failed due some unexpected hurdle. As his son became a young man and expressed a desire to climb the ladder of success, his father (out of a wish to protect his son from hurt) warned him of potential barriers. But instead of seeing this advice as positive, the son developed a fear of failure. Subsequently he passed along the same fear to his children. Families can thus create an inherent barrier to success generation after generation despite having honorable intentions. Breaking away from such a generational pattern is sometimes essential to realizing true success.

Despite being our advocates and sources of support, friends and families can impose their own self-doubts on us and create environments of negativity and fear, further hindering our determination to succeed. For these reasons I suggest acting first and revealing our successes later when it comes to friends and family. Keeping dreams and desires somewhat private and acting assertively in pursuing our goals should be our primary focus. Once we have attained various levels of success, sharing these with friends and family is fine. By then we will have developed skills and perspectives enabling us to push past obstacles and setbacks, and the potential negative influences these individuals may have will be significantly diminished. Though the road to success may involve many people, a great deal of the journey must be traveled alone. Ultimately this fosters better talents in realizing additional successes in time.

The final piece of wisdom pertaining to obstacles involves the use of other resources in pursuing our plans for success. Tapping in to outside resources can provide many advantages and should be used in many circumstances. However, when access to resources is limited, we must realize barriers can remind us of one important concept: no one is going to be as willing to risk an investment in our future as we are. Only we are able to envision our own success fully and maintain the level of determination needed to realize our dreams. Even with others who may benefit from our own personal success, their level of desire is not likely to be as great as ours. Barriers to attaining outside resources will often appear and serve as opportunities for discouragement; however, reminding ourselves that we are our best investors is important in persevering past these setbacks.

When resource barriers exist, obstacles should similarly be perceived as opportunities. Associate the obstacle with an opportunity for creativity and for the development of other success-related skills. Simply because a bank refuses to loan money for a new business or a venture capitalist demands greater proof before investing, we should not assume they have greater expertise in assessing our plans for success. Success comes from investing in ourselves and being persistent in moving toward our goals. Barriers to attaining additional resources should therefore serve to empower us to be self-reliant rather than perceiving our efforts as futile. Just because someone claims to be an expert does not mean they are knowledgeable about our own personal success potential. Remember, the creative mind can overcome any obstacle no matter what it might be.

Exercises to Overcome Obstacles and Gain Empowerment

Incorporating various exercises into your routine to help you better perceive obstacles, foster your creativity, and empower your determination can accelerate your progress toward your goals. By identifying fears and misperceptions of barriers to success, you

can choose to consider alternative viewpoints while using positive thoughts and your creative mind to make necessary shifts in
direction. At the same time, reflecting on the meaning of persistent obstacles and the various influences in your life can provide
important insights into how setbacks are being interpreted. The
following exercises can assist you in developing a positive perspective of barriers you encounter along your journey and strengthen
your abilities to overcome any obstacle you may encounter.

- *Inventory of Fears*
  (five minutes daily)
  While obstacles can arise from a variety of sources,
  fears represent a collection of common barriers that
  paralyze you and prevent you from taking action.
  The three common fears have been discussed in this
  chapter, but fear can result from any perception about
  future events that may or may not be likely to happen.
  Some fears are healthy, causing us to use a common-
  sense analysis before taking action. But others are
  exaggerated and serve only as false guides. Unless you
  routinely examine the emotions behind your hesita-
  tions, you may never realize that fear lies at the heart
  of your inaction.
  Each day as I plan my schedule and attempt
  to address current dilemmas, part of my analysis
  involves taking an inventory of my emotions and fears
  related to taking action. Why have I not yet made
  that important phone call? Why does this task seem
  always to fall last on my list of priorities? Fear can be
  subtle and sneak into your thoughts, undermining
  your determination and courage. Continue to ask
  yourself the tough questions about the real emotions

concerning a persistent obstacle to explore if some unrecognized fear exists. If it does, shed some light on that fear and determine if it indeed has merit or is actually an obstacle itself. The majority of the time, addressing your fears allows you the means to move past the barrier whether it's real or imagined.

- *Reflect on Current Obstacles*
  (ten minutes daily)
  In addition to reflecting on potential fears, examining specific roadblocks in your path should be a routine part of your daily tasks. This exercise not only involves exploring creative ways around the obstacle but also offers a moment to consider if a larger message exists. In some cases obstacles serve to guide you in a different direction that may be more productive. If you blindly persist in your planned direction without any degree of flexibility, you may miss an exceptional opportunity. By reflecting on various setbacks and obstacles (especially ones that repeatedly appear), you may realize the Creative Source is nudging you to move along a slightly different path. And if this revelation is not readily apparent, continuing to reflect patiently on an occult meaning of a persistent barrier will eventually provide you with the answer.

  As part of your daily reflection time, take a good look at various roadblocks that have occurred when you've tried to pursue various goals. Does a common theme keep surfacing? Are alternative opportunities appearing simultaneously? Is overcoming this particular obstacle a requirement to attain your success goals? Is the obstacle perhaps a test of patience, flexibility, or determination? The answers to these questions may not be immediately apparent, but in time reflecting on these issues will reveal important clues while expanding creativity, flexibility, and persistence. Commit several minutes to this exercise each day, and you will find greater meaning in each obstacle you experience.

- **Increase Your Positive-Negative Influence Ratio**
  (ten minutes weekly)
  The chance you can overcome any obstacle is directly proportional to your attitude. Through positive thinking you will attract greater creativity and determination in addition to circumstances that are more favorable to a solution. In contrast negative perceptions and doubts will inevitably lead to closed-mindedness and attract less-favorable events. In order to create environments that foster abilities to overcome barriers, you should review influences in your life on a weekly basis. We have discussed the potentially negative perspectives family members and friends can provide concerning obstacles, and situations promoting fear, failure, and a loss of confidence can do the same. By surrounding yourself with individuals who see obstacles as opportunities, your own view of obstacles will be favorably enhanced.

  Like fear, negativity can be subtle. Doubts about your ability to succeed can come from many sources. Friends, family members, spouses, and coworkers can taint your view of barriers, causing you to see them as reasons not to proceed instead of chances for growth. At least weekly, reassess interactions you had with various people and their overall influence on you. Were they encouraging and positive, or were they discouraging and negative? Did they suggest perseverance and hopefulness or resignation and hopelessness? The goal is to distance yourself from negative influences concerning barriers so you can maintain a positive perspective. As a result this will serve as a support system for empowerment, positive thinking, and growth as you continue to strive for success.

- *Consider Alternatives to Potential Setbacks* *(ten minutes weekly)* Depending on how you structure your activities for the week, performing a regular exercise to devise alternatives for various steps of your success plan can help you in several ways. First this invites the creative mind to engage in your plans for success and consider alternatives should barriers develop. Second you develop skills in flexibility and open-mindedness, which encourage positive thinking and determination. Third you reduce your fear of potential obstacles by developing solutions in advance. And last you gain greater self-confidence as you identify an array of possibilities to advance you toward your goals.

This exercise can be conducted each day or weekly, and it can also be incorporated into other activities that foster creativity. For example when I demand of myself three action steps to take each day to help me progress toward my goals, I also consider alternative options for each step in case unforeseen roadblocks develop. Alternatively, weekly reviews of your success plan could incorporate this exercise as part of a way to enrich your creative perspective and vision. Regardless of how you choose to practice this exercise, creating contingency plans develops a healthy view of approaching obstacles and ultimately success.

By perpetually seeing obstacles as opportunities and realizing their benefits to assist you toward your goals, you soon learn their important role in developing the necessary skills for continued success. Just as you need to educate yourself constantly and examine the landscape, you must also constantly examine life's challenges for potential lessons to be learned. How you perceive obstacles has a profound impact on your ability to reach your potential and your destiny of success.

Chapter Nine

Maintaining Success: Being Humble, Hungry, and Helpful

After completing law school and my adventure in the real estate market, I joined a reputable law firm as a young attorney. Life could not have been better...or so I thought. In just a few short months, I climbed through the ranks to become among the highest-paid attorneys in the firm. My energy and passion fueled my success as I strategically positioned myself as one of the rising stars within the practice. Everything seemed so natural, and success appeared to be something that easily came my way. But ignorance can be bliss. Within an even shorter period, I went from basking in my own glory to being financially and emotionally devastated. The success I had thought I would enjoy for a lifetime evaporated before my eyes. Clearly success can be a fickle companion.

During that brief yet volatile period of my life, I learned some of the most valuable lessons regarding the ability to maintain success. Three important qualities provide the necessary means by which ongoing success can be realized, and they can be succinctly summarized as humility, hunger, and helpfulness. As my income grew, so did my ego. As success was seemingly attained, I became complacent. And rather than sharing my knowledge and success with others, I hoarded my strategies of competition, keeping them to myself. Success had gone to my head, and as a result I lost it all faster than I had attained it. Nothing teaches us important lessons in life quite as well as our failures. Even if you lose, do not lose the lesson. Take what you have learned, create a new strategy, and continue upon your journey.

This time I chose to learn from my shortcomings and see my situation as an opportunity to change my life for the better. Unfortunately my story of falling from the height of success to the bottom of despair is not an uncommon one. The pitfalls I experienced are among the most common challenges people experience once attaining degrees of success. This does not mean success is necessarily difficult to perpetuate, but some simple guidelines can go a long way in helping us maintain the success we have achieved. In each instance these guidelines invoke the use of the creative mind. Just as creativity fosters our climb to the top, it likewise keeps us from falling off the cliff.

Being Humble

One of the most common pitfalls of success involves the perception we acquire of ourselves once we have made it. Having developed a plan for success and effectively realized some of our life goals, we falsely assume we have a special ability no one else has. To an extent this is true. Each of us has unique talents and skills as well as interests that align with our ultimate purpose and destiny in life. Appreciating this fact helps us realize that success is attainable by anyone. But the false perception that involves comparing our talents to others' can be detrimental. Simply because we have enjoyed some success in our life, we mistakenly believe we are in some way better than others. When this occurs the universe has a tendency to show us the error of our ways.

This lack of humility stems from the presence of a competitive mindset. Unlike the creative mind, the competitive mind sees success as being a finite and limited entity. In other words if I attain a certain degree of success, less opportunity for success subsequently exists for others to enjoy. This is particularly evident within a specific industry. From the viewpoint of the competitive mind, if my current law firm becomes reputable in dealing with hospital insurance claims, other law practices as a result will be unable to achieve a comparable position. This type of mentality naturally creates measures of accomplishment on which we gauge our success in comparison to others. Lists such as the fifty wealthiest people in the world or the top one hundred Fortune 500 companies also foster such mindsets. As we attain greater success, we acquire greater pride and ego when we ascribe to such a competitive framework.

The creative mind, in contrast, examines competition only for the purpose of seeing what needs and wants exist within a market. If one competitor is providing a specific type of product or service, the creative mind will consider a variation or twist in that concept in developing a completely new offering. Perhaps another attorney providing legal services that are similar to mine develops a service specific to natural-disaster insurance claims while representing homeowners. Rather than competing with me, he or she has chosen to use creativity to develop a similar service for another area of the market. The creative mind seeks to identify unmet needs and develop value through products and services that meet those needs. As a result the focus is on value creation rather than on competition.

The ability to focus on needs of the community and various markets reflects a service-oriented approach to success. Where the competitive mind boasts one's skills and talents in achieving success, the creative mind constantly asks how it can be of service to others. This latter perspective embraces humility rather than pride, which is an important asset in perpetuating success. The creative mind pushes us to become the best versions of ourselves rather than seeking to acquire a particular figure of wealth or status position. Our goals may include such figures or positions, but our perspective is not solely focused on these items alone. Instead we should identify our drive, passion, and purpose while applying creativity and positive thinking. Our goals of wealth and/or fame will still be achieved, but they will be realized through creative expression and enhancement of value instead of through competitive techniques. And in the process, we are likely to remain humble instead of prideful.

Maintaining humility in light of success can be accomplished by investing in a creative mindset instead of a competitive perspective. Many of the activities outlined in this book help us keep this viewpoint, but at the same time we must surround ourselves with reminders and influences promoting humility. As I have attained various levels of success, I have realized humility can be threatened by the comments of others. Being aware of new people who come into our lives after we attain success is important. Often these individuals seek to usurp our energy and creativity for their own purposes. More importantly they routinely use compliments and flattery as a means to ingratiate themselves with us. This latter strategy can serve to fuel our ego at the expense of being humble. In addition to such relationships lacking depth and value, they may also foster a more competitive mindset which will ultimately weaken our chances for continued success.

In addition to cultivating a creative mindset and surrounding myself with healthy influences, I regularly reflect on my past as a means to remain humble. Remembering how quickly my success came and went as a young attorney deepens my respect for achievement in general while helping me appreciate my inherent source of creation that remains untapped. Likewise the lessons I learned as a result of those experiences provoke feelings of thankfulness and graciousness. Remembering my childhood and the struggles we survived as a family empower me, and at the same time these memories promote appreciation for accomplishments I have attained in my life. By remembering our roots and our history, we maintain an awareness of who we are in addition to the limitations and weaknesses others have placed upon us and our ability to overcome them. These serve to keep us grounded and encourage us to keep striving to become better and better. This leads us to our second strategy in maintaining success: keeping a hunger for continued growth.

Keeping a Hunger

One of the biggest problems in maintaining success involves the development of complacency. After reaching some of our success milestones and goals, a tendency to lose determination in completing the journey can occur. When we become complacent, we lose track of our purpose and direction. We ignore our natural need to evolve continually and grow as individuals. In part this need to grow and change emanates from within, but similarly our environments constantly demand change as well. If we refuse to embrace ongoing change within ourselves, we will likely see success slowly (or sometimes rapidly) slip through our fingers. For this reason maintaining a hunger for growth is essential for continued success.

Recently my wife and I had dinner with a couple who had moved from New York City a few months earlier. As the conversation progressed, the woman repeatedly expressed how unhappy she was with their relocation to Miami. She criticized the climate, complained about a lack of friends, and described several activities she had enjoyed in New York but were lacking in her new environment. But as the evening continued, it became evident these issues had little to do with her unhappiness. As the mother of two small children and with no other career, she lacked a sense of purpose in life, and with this loss of purpose she had likewise lost her passion. Without the means to grow and evolve, she had become stagnant and, as a result, dissatisfied. Regardless of where she lived, her unhappiness was likely to stay until she addressed the real problem. After uncovering this hidden truth in my conversation with this new acquaintance, the woman's husband turned to me and said, "You tapped in to a hidden power, didn't you?"

Even if we have attained success, the ability to remain fulfilled demands we continue to pursue our own passions and desires. As we reach specific milestones, our passions and desires may change and grow as well. Because of this, goals may change in time. Past success does not guarantee continued success. Each of us must maintain a passion of purpose in order to perpetuate success moving forward. This is accomplished through the creative mind, which seeks to enhance our lives and the lives of others through value creation. By taking something in which we believe and applying creative energies to that belief, we naturally continue to grow. We eventually come to realize that goals are not the objects of our fulfillment but the actual journey itself. Through creativity and the development of new ideas, we receive our greatest joy as well as our greatest success. Therefore hunger for continued success is intimately connected to happiness, personal fulfillment, and our inner passions.

Amazing things happen when we apply our creative mind to an underlying personal desire and sense of purpose. Fewer than six months ago, I approached an entertainment arena about creating a concert for the purpose of a charitable fundraiser. I was passionate about the project because I truly wanted to raise food donations for my charity. As usual a few obstacles stood in the way. I knew absolutely nothing about the entertainment industry and even less about the organization and promotion of a concert. But rather than allow this to deter my efforts, I embraced the opportunity. My creative mind began to look for opportunities to enhance value and meet unfulfilled needs.

In speaking with more-knowledgeable individuals in the entertainment industry, I learned most arena concert events cost between $300,000 and $400,000 and profit approximately $75,000 if all goes well. Of course this traditional approach carries significant risk, which I was not willing to take. With a creative approach and positive thinking, I devised a completely new paradigm for the concert, its schedule of events, and its funding. A comprehensive preshow, advanced sponsorships, social media streaming, and merchandising were used to reduce risk while creating greater hype for the venue. I examined the landscape and added value where I saw a need existed. Today I am not only much more knowledgeable about concert events but am reinventing how future events will be conducted. Not bad for a guy who had yet to attend a concert.

As a successful attorney, educator, and businessperson, I could have chosen to be complacent rather than to pursue a new area of interest. But the creative mind never rests. The creative mind seeks to grow, evolve, and expand. It remains hungry for creating new concepts and ideas and turning them into reality. When we embrace creativity and positive thinking, we have little difficulty finding a perpetual fountain of interests and passions. Regardless of the success we have already attained, we remain energized to learn, create, and expand in areas we have yet to explore. All we need to do is allow our creative mind to take control. Through it and the natural law of attraction, we will continue to bring continued success our way.

In staying hungry for continued success, a never-ending desire to grow undermines everything we do. With this in mind, the possibility of growing too quickly could threaten what we have already established. Spreading ourselves too thin by investing in future successes with past accomplishments could place us in a weakened position. Gauging our growth is certainly good advice, but despite an awareness of these warnings, I commonly push forward regardless. Is it because I am being reckless or careless? Or am I defiant in my desire to succeed? Perhaps the latter explanation is closer to the truth, but my determination to grow and expand stems from my faith in my creative mind and in the Creative Source to guide me. In addition I have learned that spreading one's endeavors into a variety of areas can actually be a method of success protection.

Diversification simply means not placing all our eggs in one basket. By maintaining multiple lines of income or success, we safeguard our position. If one endeavor suddenly falters, several others are still viable. Consider my entertainment company for example. Suppose that just before the concert, an unexpected hurricane strikes the coast of Florida, resulting in cancellation of the show. Without question a significant return on my investment would become an impossibility. But with such an event, the media coverage and public relations associated the hurricane and concert cancellation were likely to be significant. As one of the major sponsors of the event, Celler Law PA would receive widespread marketing exposure, exposing new clients to the firm. Even if the concert has a major setback, my law practice will reap some benefits, allowing other avenues of success.

Diversification is a great way to remain hungry and continue our expansion toward broader areas of success while protecting ourselves from risk. While we need to be cognizant of the pace at which we expand, having multiple areas of interest helps us realize greater success while encouraging passion. By having a variety of passions, we maintain a level of excitement, keeping us hungry for increased success. Through novelty and constant learning, we remain energized to embrace our creative mind instead of becoming bored and complacent. Ultimately we realize success is not about the end result but instead about the creative journey. Once this is appreciated, staying hungry becomes second nature as we enthusiastically pursue new endeavors and foster continued growth.

Being Helpful

When we think about success in any form, we naturally envision abundance. If we consider financial wealth as a means of success, we likely perceive an abundance of money with which we can acquire many wonderful things. If we consider status and notoriety as success, our perception probably involves widespread recognition among many different people. Success, like creativity, is indeed abundant in nature. For this reason alone, the path to success demands creativity over competition. When resources are limited, competition occurs so the finite amount can be distributed according to some allocation measure. However, success is unlimited, expansive, and infinite. While many individuals falsely perceive success as a limited commodity, it is actually plentiful because success relies on creativity. Because our creative mind offers infinite resources, opportunities for success are similarly unlimited.

In understanding the abundance of creativity and success, we soon realize we have the potential to share our success with others and empower them as well. Creativity not only fosters growth and expansion within ourselves, but it also aids in facilitating growth and accomplishments around us. Increasingly we develop a desire to share our knowledge and strategies with others. We begin to employ our creative mind in areas other than our own personal success so we may help fulfill social needs. The topic of corporate social responsibility has become prominent in many business discussions today. In some instances a push for greater ethical character and values within organizations has been encouraged in light of recent corporate scandals. But for other companies, the realization that creativity and success are in surplus is driving their desire to give back to their communities.

If we consider the power of the creative mind, we soon realize creativity itself is more powerful and more valuable than any form of actual success. After all is the fish worth more than the skill of fishing? In fact applying creativity toward efforts to help others provides numerous rewards that are usually under-recognized. Consider a business investing in new procedures to recycle their production byproducts. Creative ways are employed to change operational workflows, allowing the recycling to occur. Secondarily, greenhouse gas emissions are reduced since the purchase and transportation of new materials drop significantly. The social benefit is achieved by improving the environment, but simultaneously the company becomes more efficient, reduces its expenses, and realizes greater profits. In many creative endeavors, multiple stakeholders receive benefits because of the creative mind's inclusive nature.

Maintaining success can be greatly enhanced by a desire to help others and share one's success. Interestingly, when we begin to follow such a path, we rarely know where the road may end. In most cases the journey exceeds our expectations. I had one such journey that started only six months ago. While I was with my family on vacation, my niece showed me a photograph of a donut company discarding bags of unsold donuts into the trash at the end of the day. Having grown up in a household struggling to place food on the table, the image struck me as incredibly wasteful. I could just imagine how many other food organizations and restaurants did the same despite the number of people in need of food. Within minutes I was creatively trying to solve the problem and devise a way I might help improve the situation. My goal had nothing to do with personal success. I simply wanted to use my creative mind to help solve a social need.

After returning from vacation, I educated myself about the food industry and visited a few food distribution centers. In essence a missing link existed between restaurants and the food distribution centers. A method to transport the food in a timely manner was not in place. Food distribution centers lacked the resources to finance trucks and drivers, and restaurants lacked incentives due to potential liabilities and the costs involved in packing the food for donation. With the passage of Good Samaritan laws relieving restaurants of any food-related liabilities related to donation, I formed the Bobbie Celler Feeds the World foundation, which provides a truck and a part-time driver for food distribution centers to use throughout the greater South Florida area. In addition the foundation offers to pay restaurants small purchase amounts for their unused food to help incentivize their donations. With a bit of creativity, a significant need was filled within the market, and many individuals now benefit from this vision of success.

While this story of my foundation depicts how creativity can serve others, it also demonstrates how creativity is ever expansive. As a means of promoting the foundation's efforts, I did an interview appearance on *The Daily Buzz* on the CW Network. This resulted eventually in the opportunity to host my own program on the network to provide legal expertise. In addition my conversations with various food distribution centers identified a need for canned foods in addition to the unused foods we harvested. This led to the creation of an evening fundraising event called Rock the Plate that provided rock, hip-hop, and country music entertainment at a local town, which then evolved into a top-40 music concert involving numerous artists at the BB&T center. The event will include a preshow festival in the afternoon where only three cans of food will be required as the admission price. Additionally, efforts in planning this event evolved into a halftime extravaganza in partnership with Jon Secada, which consists of a talent audition, a Halloween costume contest, and a scream contest. From a wasted bag of donuts to Bobbie Celler's Screamfest, the infusion of creativity and a desire to help others in need opened doors I would have been unlikely to pursue. When we strive to help and do well, the Creative Source listens and rewards us in exponential proportion.

Looking back I find it amazing how the creative mind expanded opportunities in my life in such a short time. Some people ask why I chose to invest my own money in the foundation rather than seek public grants. Certainly the foundation developed programs that would have qualified for government assistance. But ultimately these grants come from monies collected from taxes and represent public resources. I wanted to give to others personally out of the abundance of my own successes. If I had viewed success as a competition where some individuals win and some lose, I would have been less likely to give away my own resources, feeling this would have made me somehow vulnerable. But in viewing success as a product of creativity, I wanted to share myself and my successes with others.

The other primary reason for refusing grants and other sources of money involves the restriction of creativity. When public assistance is provided, oversight and approval of the funds are often required. Unfortunately such processes often impose restrictions and limits that naturally hinder one's creativity. The creative mind enjoys freedoms without rules and restrictions. It needs an environment to explore a variety of possibilities. By giving of myself, I maintain this atmosphere of freedom and foster enhanced creativity and exploration of ideas. Without the imposition of oversight, I can offer unique solutions to complex problems free of someone second guessing their practicality or rationale. If we have faith in our creative mind and believe in its ability to create success, we can confidently share ourselves with others without fear.

Helping others is an important aspect of maintaining success because it is an opportunity for us to demonstrate our faith and confidence in our creative mind. Helping also embraces the concept of limitlessness and abundance of success, which is available to everyone. When we use our creative abilities and leverage the universal law of attraction to help others, we expand and grow personally in our abilities to be successful. And often we are greatly rewarded for our efforts as our creativity invites new opportunities for ongoing successes in our lives. Helping others by donating money may be fine, but ultimately knowing where such donations go and how they are used can be difficult. But in using the creative mind to help fulfill a need, we not only see the fruits of our labor but also benefit from them personally as well.

Exercises to Stay Humble, Hungry, and Helpful

Each of the key qualities to help you maintain success stem from an ability to foster a creative mindset. The creative mind is naturally humble, envisioning vast opportunities yet to be realized. The magnitude of such a vision inherently fosters humility. Likewise the creative mind continually seeks growth and expansion, which develops a passionate hunger to improve and progress constantly. And the creative mind enjoys sharing itself with others knowing the possibilities for success are without limits. The more you develop a creative mind, the more likely it will be that you can avoid many common pitfalls associated with success.

- ***Reflect on Improving Past Performance***
  (fifteen minutes weekly)
  Success allows you two primary choices: you can reflect on your achievements and the positive aspects allowing you to excel, or you can focus on various missteps occurring along the way. Both can be beneficial as the former promotes positive thinking and confidence, and the latter allows you to examine areas of weakness that may be improved. In an effort to enhance both your creative mindset and your humility, reflecting on areas for improvement offers the greatest value. By examining your flaws and vulnerabilities, you remain humble and acknowledge that current success does not indicate perpetual success. And by seeking to improve these weaknesses, you engage your creative mind.

  This exercise can be performed in combination with various other activities outlined in this book. When you reflect on goals, setbacks, or new strategies, you may choose also to reflect on past performances and areas for improvement. Alternatively you may implement this activity as part of your planning process to help identify more-effective strategies. Once you attain some level of success, this activity should be a dedicated part of your routine performed at least weekly. Humility is something to be treasured, and identifying areas where you are less than perfect can be helpful in this regard.

- ***Invest in Personal Growth***
  (new activity at least monthly)
  Every living entity seeks to grow and expand. Even upon maturity plants as well as animals continue to grow as they strive to survive. We even label aging as "growing old" instead of "becoming old." So the desire to grow is quite natural and expresses an innate quality of all living things. Your desire to be successful represents this same instinct to expand and broaden your abilities, skills, and achievements. Therefore when you choose to become complacent with your current levels of achievement, you are actually behaving in opposition to your human nature. Instead you should continually seek to grow and create, and in turn this will allow your hunger to remain alive.

  People choose to grow and expand their abilities in different ways. Some considerations may involve formal education, new hobbies, entrepreneurial pursuits, and sudden changes in lifestyles. Any of these may offer you opportunities for growth, but the important aspect is to combine novelty with passion. Choose to pursue new interests that inspire you and motivate you. This will help create a hunger for additional success and maintain a growth perspective. Any endeavor that makes you feel a bit uncomfortable but also filled with excitement is likely to reflect a great opportunity to keep your hunger for success healthy and alive.

- ### *Diversify Pursuits*
  (assess risk weekly—ten minutes)
  Diversifying your pursuits of success offers many advantages. In addition to protecting your success by reducing risk, diversification also fosters a creative mind as it explores new opportunities for growth and success. This aspect enhances your hunger for continued achievement. Likewise diversification helps you remain humble since you are less likely to be as confident and knowledgeable when examining new opportunities. This growth mindset, which is constantly learning and gathering new information, reminds you that you indeed do not know it all! Lastly, if done with creativity and a service-oriented mindset, diversification will seek to help others while adding to personal achievements. In every aspect diversification allows us to maintain success.

  The other activities promoting creativity will naturally encourage a diverse range of interests, passions, and pursuits. But in addition, assessing your risk on a weekly basis can help you gauge your current level of diversification. Ask yourself questions that expose risk and a need for greater variety in your pursuits. What will happen if my current market collapses next week? What if a sudden technological shift makes my current success obsolete? If one of my current successes collapses, will my other achievements provide security and stability? The purpose of these questions is not to induce fear or negative thoughts but to encourage creative efforts to explore new areas of growth. By assessing risk, a need for enhanced diversification can be revealed.

- ***Identify Needs and Value Opportunities***
  (fifteen minutes weekly)
  Exploration lies at the heart of creativity. The creative mind is continually seeking to add value to existing success and fulfill ongoing needs everywhere. You can foster both hunger and helpfulness by regularly assessing your current activities for new opportunities and ways to improve upon existing performance. Likewise you can expand and grow by staying attentive to potential needs within the marketplace and throughout your community. Creativity leading to success has no boundaries between business and life. The creative mind remains vigilant in its search to always enhance life in every way possible.

  Each and every day, you should remind yourself that success is a limitless resource. If needed, develop a mantra to help reinforce this notion so you may be empowered to share your success and creativity with others. Once this is accomplished, be diligent in looking for ways to improve your own actions, your own successes, and the lives of others around you. Share your time, knowledge, and success with others, helping them adopt a creative mindset as well. At least weekly, devote a dedicated period of time to consider ways in which you can enhance value and share your success with others. As a result you will become even more creative and enjoy ever-expanding success.

The ability to maintain success to a large extent emanates from persisting in your efforts to grow, expand, and become the very best version of yourself. Such practices are fostered when you surround yourself with positive influences and cultivate a creative mind. The creative mind is humble, understanding success is accessible to all, and as a result this mindset enthusiastically shares success through helping others. With continued success you will also appreciate that the process of creating actually harbors the greatest pleasures in life. This in turn allows you to stay hungry not only for future successes but for the purpose of creating. The best way to maintain success is therefore to embrace the creative mindset continually no matter what levels of achievement have been attained.

Chapter Ten

The Creative Mind:
The Nine Essentials

Having journeyed through the chapters of this book, we now have the tools needed to realize the success each of us can achieve in our lives. By describing the integral nature of the creative mind in materializing our dreams and ideas, the secret to attaining tremendous success has been revealed. Creativity lies at the heart of our ascent and is also essential to continued achievements thereafter. The creative mind seeks to grow and expand constantly regardless of the goals attained because progress remains the essence of life. Our destiny awaits us, and all we must do is embrace our own potential through exercising our creative mind.

As a means of review, nine key elements characterize the creative mind. Each builds upon the other, and when combined in total, unlimited success awaits us. Some establish a solid foundation upon which success may build just as the hull of a ship must be constructed in a way that prevents leaks and submersion. Others serve to guide and direct our course in an efficient and productive fashion, overcoming obstacles and learning lessons from them along the way. And still others serve to fuel our vessel, empowering us to persevere through calm and stormy waters alike. Each has the potential to push us further as we move toward our destination, but tapping in to all of these at once enables the creative mind to thrive, and we soon find our ability to excel enhanced exponentially.

While the prior chapters of the book discussed these characteristics of the creative mind in detail along with core activities to help us develop them in our daily lives, a summary will be presented along with a sample schedule designed to help you achieve your goals accordingly. Just as our individual dreams and desires are uniquely different from others', so too will be our schedules for achieving success. Consider the sample provided, and then create one best suited to that uniqueness. Regardless of how activities are arranged, the same core elements of the creative mind hold the key to attaining success. Of all the many resources on earth, creativity is one of the few limitless ones. Because of this very fact, the creative mind offers us the pathway to make our dreams of success come true no matter how large you wish to dream!

The Nine Core Elements of the Creative Mind

- *Positive thinking*—Positive thoughts generate favorable psychic energies that in turn attract other positive developments in our lives. Through the law of attraction, we soon attract success into our lives as positive thoughts stimulate the creative mind and provide it with energy to grow, expand, and create. Instead of seeing closed doors ahead, we realize new opportunities aligned with our desires for success. Likewise positive thinking helps us connect with the Creative Source, which directs us along the most-efficient and most-productive paths as we seek greater achievements. Though we may not always see a tangible connection between positive thoughts and successes, both science and religion are recognizing this important link. If we wish to encourage the development of the creative mind, we must start with positive thinking and the law of attraction.

• *Limitless dreaming*—The creative mind is expansive, and the ability to dream without limits reflects its vast open-mindedness. Creativity demands imagination, consideration of the impossible, and exploration of unchartered territories. If we approach challenges with perceived limits, fears, and boundaries, we handcuff our chances to fulfill our destiny and realize our greatest dreams. When we unshackle ourselves from these restraints and free our minds from any limits, innovative possibilities appear. Allowing ourselves the ability to dream and dream big enables our creative minds to explore strategies naturally to turn them into reality. In addition dreaming enables us to connect more completely with the ultimate Creative Source, which also desires for us to fulfill our greatest potential. Our successes can only be as grand as our capacity to dream. To realize tremendous success, we must encourage our creative mind to explore the depths of our imagination and find those dreams that arouse the greatest passions within us.

• *Visualizing success*—Just as psychic energies and the law of attraction lack tangibility, the creative mind often operates without conscious awareness. At a subconscious level, the creative mind explores solutions to problems and connects with the Creative Source. And a great deal of information and mental inputs (which typically go unnoticed) can have profound effects on the creative mind and on our opportunities for success. Visualizations, and specifically vision boards, offer powerful ways for us to feed our creative mind with positive energies aligned with dreams of success. A picture is worth a thousand words, and providing visual images of our dreams offers rich material with which the creative mind can work. The more visualizations we provide, the greater the capacity to engage our subconscious and creative mental energies. This often poorly utilized resource is an important strategy to empower the creative mind.

- *Holistic preparation*—Much of the discussion about the creative mind involves specific aspects of mental activities designed to enhance creativity, growth, and expansion. But we are not simply thinking and dreaming machines. Physically, spiritually, and mentally we are interconnected, and each aspect contributes to the whole. Holistic preparation of the body, mind, and spirit is thus necessary to enable the creative mind to reach its greatest potential. Dedicating time to physical exercise, eating proper nutrition in proper portions, and getting adequate rest and personal time bolster our creative abilities. Spending time in quiet stillness and spiritual reflection allows for growth and expansion. And continually learning and attaining knowledge enhance idea formation. To develop the best environment in which the creative mind can excel, a holistic approach to healthy preparation goes a long way.

- *Belief, faith, and determination*—Having prepared the vehicle and identified our destination, we need fuel to power us through the journey. Determination and willpower provide this fuel and enable us to persevere despite obstacles and fears. As we identify and pursue our passions, we naturally become energized in our efforts to realize success. Through positive thinking and support provided by the law of attraction, we gain increasing amounts of belief and faith in our abilities to fulfill our dreams. These aspects form the foundation of determination and perseverance. When we are passionate about a pursuit, believe we can achieve a goal and have faith in ourselves and the universe—nothing can stop us. Likewise, reflecting on past successes and seeking inspiration from others strengthen our will. Determination is perhaps the single most powerful feature of success-driven individuals. Combine this trait with the other components of the creative mind, and no obstacle can prevent success from being realized.

- *Detailed planning*—While the creative mind provides great opportunities to attract circumstances that foster the realization of success, planning remains an important part of the process. In fact the creative mind, when engaged in success-planning goals, offers unique and powerful insights we otherwise might miss. Whether success involves a specific career or entrepreneurial pursuits, creating a detailed roadmap equipped with specific goals and deadlines provides the necessary guidance and accountability needed for attaining goals. Likewise, planning gives us the chance to develop our branding and explore marketing of either ourselves or our business. While we often lack the ability to see the details on the distant horizon, having a success plan in place gives us the necessary structure for action, an essential ingredient in attaining success. The road to success is lined with dreamers who failed to plan and to act in accordance with their ideas. For the creative mind to be realized fully, success planning remains an essential tool.

- *Fast, focused, faithful, and flexible*—With a success plan in place, working it with our creative mind requires us to be efficient, productive, dedicated, and adaptable. As we pursue our goals, we must determine how we can best utilize the resources we have available. We need to minimize distractions and stay on task. We must diligently follow our plans every day, striving to make constant progress. And we should be ready to adapt and change as obstacles and setbacks as well as new opportunities present themselves. Our ability to work our plans effectively for success depends on these four characteristics. By employing the creative mind in this regard, we are continually improving our skills and abilities to attain our goals and realize success. New ways to become more efficient and productive are devised, and creative ways to adapt and remained focused despite various roadblocks progressively improve. Not only is the creative mind important in envisioning success, but it remains a necessary instrument in working toward our dreams and goals.

- *Growing through obstacles*—We often tend to fear obstacles and setbacks, and when they occur we can lose momentum in our pursuit of success. The creative mind, however, fails to see obstacles as roadblocks or hindrances but instead sees them as opportunities for growth and expansion. Through challenges we are forced to use creativity and innovation to develop alternatives. Developing contingency plans offers exercises that foster our talents in adaptation, persistence, and faithfulness. Likewise, obstacles test our ability to use positive thinking and creative reflection to overcome potential barriers. Each of these strengthens our creative mind in its journey to gain success. Along the way we progressively acquire wisdom and knowledge, which benefit us in future challenges. In time the fear and anxiety we may have initially experienced with various setbacks transform into feelings of excitement as we perceive additional chances to be creative. No one who has ever enjoyed long-term success did so without overcoming obstacles, and ultimately these challenges serve to enhance our creative mind and aid us in achieving our goals.

- *Being humble, hungry, and helpful*—Finally, the creative mind is also important in maintaining success once achieved. In many circumstances individuals who attain success lose it within a short time. Pitfalls can include becoming prideful, losing one's desire for continued growth, and focusing on goals that are detrimental to ongoing success. Three key activities help us maintain success: the ability to stay humble, stay hungry, and be helpful. Through humility we maintain a growth mindset that is necessary for continued expansion and creativity. By continually identifying our desires and passions, we retain a hunger for ongoing success. And through charitable efforts to share our success with others, we keep a perspective that is consistent with a creative mind rather than a competitive one. A creative mindset is always pursuing growth, expansion, and achievement, and it perceives an unlimited potential for success for everyone. Humility, hunger, and helpfulness are core traits that help us maintain a creative mind no matter how much success we experience.

When reviewing these essential characteristics of the creative mind, certain terms come to mind such as *growth, positive thinking, creativity, expansiveness, adaptability,* and *liberation.* Indeed the creative mindset is one that constantly sees opportunities without boundaries and as a result promotes inclusion instead of exclusion. By committing to the activities outlined in this book that foster the creative mind, anyone can achieve whatever level of success they desire. I am living proof the creative mind provides the means by which success can be attained and maintained. Success rarely happens overnight, and long-term success always demands these principles be followed. When you make the decision to adopt these traits as part of your life, significant changes will occur in a short amount of time, and ultimately success will be realized beyond expectation.

Imagine if everyone chose to commit to the practices in this book. Think of the advancements we would make as a society and as a global population! Being a limitless resource, creativity offers the chance to attain incredible success to us not only as individuals but also as a global community. You now know the secret to true success starts and ends with the creative mind, and the creative mind seeks to empower everyone and everything. Each action seeks to enhance value while meeting ongoing needs, and in the process self-fulfillment is attained. I challenge you to take this information to change your life for the better and pursue the level of success you were destined to achieve. Likewise, I challenge you to share this knowledge and your story with everyone in your life. By accomplishing this, we all will be amazed by the potential and power the creative mind has to offer for us all.

Success Schedule Sample

Weekday Mornings (Three Hours of Power)
4:30 a.m.–7:30 a.m.

- *4:30 a.m.–5:30 a.m.:* Daily physical exercise, 30-60 minutes

- *5:30 a.m.–6:30 a.m.:* Reflection and inspirational exercises
  - Inspirational readings: 10 minutes
  - Research new inspirations: 10 minutes
  - Explore passions: 5 minutes
  - Inventory of fears: 5 minutes
  - Positive affirmations: 5 minutes
  - Shift expectations: 5 minutes
  - Study vision board: 5 minutes
  - Quiet stillness: 15 minutes

- *6:30 a.m.–7:30 a.m.:* Action plans for daily success exercises
  - Reflect on current obstacles: 10 minutes
  - Efficiency inventory: 10 minutes
  - Brainstorming: 10 minutes
  - Three ideas for progress: 10 minutes
  - Positive actions to take: 5 minutes

- One percent shift in progress: 5 minutes
- Develop contingencies for success-plan goals: 10 minutes

Weekday Evenings *8:00 p.m.–9:00 p.m.*
- *8:00 p.m.–9:00 p.m.*: Daily journaling and study
  - Study vision board: 5 minutes
  - Journaling: 15 minutes
  - Study and knowledge preparation: 30 minutes
  - Distancing plans for negative influences: 5 minutes
  - Seeds for sleep: 5 minutes

Weekly Activities *(Weekends, total of 3 hours)*
- Creative escape: 1 hour
- Feed mind creative images: 10 minutes
- Reflect on recent successes and failures: 15 minutes
- Reflect on long-term positive and negative influences: 10 minutes
- Identify areas of needed self-control: 10 minutes
- Review deadlines: 10 minutes
- Reevaluate and refine brand: 15 minutes
- Devise ways to improve past performance: 15 minutes
- Develop long-range plan alternatives: 10 minutes
- Assess level of diversification and risks: 10 minutes
- Identify market needs and opportunities to enhance value: 15 minutes

Monthly Activities
- Revise vision board
- Reflect on past vision boards
- Reward perseverance
- Reexamine drives for success
- Invest in personal growth through new experiences

Annual Activities
- Business/career plan review and revision

Endnotes

1   Hill, Napoleon. *Think and Grow Rich: The Original Classic.* Capstone, 2011.

2   Byrne, Rhonda. *The Secret.* Atria Books, 2006.

3   Fredrickson, Barbara. *Positivity: Top-Notch Research Reveals the 3 to 1 Ratio That Will Change Your Life.* Three Rivers Press, 2009.

4   Ibid.

5   Ibid.

6   Wattles, Wallace D. *The Science of Getting Rich.* Atria Books/ Beyond Words, 2007.

7   Ibid.

8   Byrne, 2006.

9   Moore, Elizabeth Armstrong. "Human brain has more switches than all computers on Earth." *CNET,* November 17 (2010).

10   Feil, Robert, and Mario F. Fraga. "Epigenetics and the environment: emerging patterns and implications." *Nature Reviews Genetics* 13, no. 2 (2012): 97-109.

11   Stallone, Sylvester. *Rocky III.* Film. Director Sylvester Stallone. Los Angeles: MGM/UA Entertainment Company, 1982.

12   Hill, 2011.

13   Fredrickson, 2009.

14   Buckworth, Janet, Rod Dishman, Patrick J. O'Connor, and Phillip Tomporowski. *Exercise Psychology.* Human Kinetics Publishers, 2013.

15   Hill, 2011.

16   Emerson, Ralph Waldo. *The Essential Writings of Ralph Waldo Emerson.* Modern library, 2009.

17   Barkley, Russell A. *Attention-deficit Hyperactivity Disorder and the Nature of Self-control.* Guilford Press, 1997.

18   Romney, Lee. "Personal car-sharing is a new twist on auto rentals." *Los Angeles Times,* Feb 12, 2012.

About the Author

CEO, Attorney, Author, TV Host, Radio Host, Concert Promoter, Motivational Speaker, Philanthropist

As Chairman of the Board, Founder, and CEO, Bobbie Celler is at the helm of The Celler Organization, which consists of Celler Law P.A., EPS-Global, Healthcare Billing Solutions, Emergency Recovery, Celler Entertainment, Empower Design, and Bobbie Celler Feeds The World Foundation.

The Celler Organization is designed to help all businesses by implementing cutting-edge solutions to promote efficiency, reduce costs, and significantly increase revenue. In 2012 the Celler Law, P.A. company generated approximately $20 million in insurance reimbursements for mostly nonprofit hospitals, for which patients otherwise would have been responsible.

Bobbie Celler is also a TV Host on the nationally syndicated show *The Daily Buzz* on The CW Network and Life, Love, Shopping (LLS) on Oxygen Cable Network.

Many peers and colleagues refer to Mr. Celler as an "inventor of business models". He visualizes business models in a different array of industries and persists until he converts those ideas into tangible and concrete results. Bobbie Celler is the very definition of the American success story. He has continually set new standards of excellence while expanding his interests nationally and internationally.